Indian Village Revisited

Indian Village Revisited

Ranawaton-ki-Sadri (1955–2005)

Brij Raj Chauhan

Edited by
Yogesh Atal

Institute of Social Development, Udaipur

RAWAT PUBLICATIONS
Jaipur • New Delhi • Bangalore • Guwahati • Kolkata

ISBN 978-81-316-0926-2

Published in association with
Institute of Social Development
49, Mahaveer Nagar, Sector 4, Hiran Magri,
Udaipur 313 002 (Rajasthan)
Ph.: 0294-2461079
E-mail: isdu2001@yahoo.co.in

Published by
Prem Rawat for **Rawat Publications**
Satyam Apts., Sector 3, Jawahar Nagar, Jaipur 302 004 (India)
Phone: 0141 265 1748 / 7006 Fax: 0141 265 1748
E-mail: info@rawatbooks.com
Website: www.rawatbooks.com

New Delhi Office
4858/24, Ansari Road, Daryaganj, New Delhi 110 002
Phone: 011-23263290

Also at *Bangalore, Guwahati* and *Kolkata*

Typeset by Rawat Computers, Jaipur
Printed at Chaman Enterprises, New Delhi

Contents

Preliminaries

The Book: *Indian Village Revisited*

Obituaries and Tributes

Preliminaries

Prologue

T.M. Dak

Present book titled *Indian Village Revisited* is authored by Professor Brij Raj Chauhan. After a lapse of nearly fifty years, Professor Chauhan chose to revisit the village to see how the village has transformed during the interregnum. The Indian Council of Social Science Research waived the condition of the age limit of the applicant and gave the generous grant for the project to employ some investigators and meet other expenses. In getting ICSSR's financial support for this project, Professor Yogesh Atal and Professor Abha Avasthi played a crucial role.

The project was carried out under the auspices of the Institute of Social Development, Udaipur. The first study of the village carried out by Professor Chauhan in the 1950s was published by Vir Publishing House, New Delhi in 1967. Its subsequent editions were published by A.C. Brothers. The fact that the original study had three editions speaks of the high reception of that monograph.

Professor Chauhan ventured to restudy the village again after a gap of about half a century. Despite his failing health, he himself undertook several visits to the village and personally interviewed the village potentates. Both the author and the respondents nostalgically recalled the village life of the olden days. His visits also served an encouragement to the field team working under his guidance.

Because of his ill health, Professor Chauhan was keen to complete the write-up using the computer. He succeeded in his fight due to his strong will power and completed the monograph. He immediately sent a copy to Professor Yogesh Atal, one of his prodigies with the remark that he has kept his promise. Alas, he had to yield to the divine call and finally left the world on 3 November 2009. We are glad that this book, though late, is being published on the 8th Death Anniversary of Professor Chauhan. We pay our tributes to the departed soul.

Since the Project was carried out under the auspices of the Udaipur based Institute of Social Development, we were keen to get this study published. Finally it was in 2016 – when Professor Yogesh Atal came to Udaipur to receive the award from the Rajasthan Sociological Society – I had a chance to raise this matter with him. Both of us have been Professor Chauhan's students and are class fellows. He readily agreed to my suggestion to undertake the editing of the monograph. He views this assignment as "*Guru Dakshina*".

As a posthumous publication, we could not have found a better person to do the needed editing and polishing. The finishing touches given by Professor Atal has improved the readability of the book. Upon my request, Professor Atal has kindly contributed a long *Prolegomenon* to the book which assesses the contribution of Professor Chauhan as pioneer in introducing teaching of Sociology in Rajasthan. His students both from Rajasthan, and later from Uttar Pradesh, have made noted contributions to Indian Sociology. This being a posthumous publication, had offered an opportunity to annex tributes to the author by some of his dear students. That gives us an occasion to publish the obituary written by Professor Yogesh Atal who has also done the prolegomenon. That piece is a supplement but a useful document to reproduce.

My choice for Professor Atal was mainly guided by the fact that he was his student. I had a chance discovery of an article that Professor Chauhan had written in the Festschrift done in his honour, and published by Messrs Concept Publishing House, titled *Emerging Social Science Concerns* (2004). I thought it advisable to quote from his essay. This would be the unique way of presenting the teacher and the student together.

In addition to Professor Yogesh Atal, I wish to put on record the generous contributions made by some of the closest students and admirers of Professor Chauhan to facilitate publication of this book and to institute an annual lecture in his memory in collaboration with organisations such as the Rajasthan Sociological Society. Their contribution is a token of their regard for their revered teacher who laid the foundations of teaching Sociology in Rajasthan and for shaping their careers.

On behalf of the Institute, I would also wish to specially thank Professor Satyanarayana Alturi (former Vice Chancellor of Allahabad University), Prof. Surendra Munshi (retired Professor of IIM, Kolkata), Professor Abha Chauhan (daughter of Professor Chauhan, and currently the Member-Secretary of the Indian Sociological Society),

Professor Giri Raj Gupta (retired Professor of Sociology at Western Illinois University, USA), Mr Stig Toft Medsen, Senior Researcher, NIAS, Nordic Institute of Asian Studies, Copenhagen, Denmark, Dr. Kuntal Agarwal (Faculty Member of Department of Sociology, Raghunath Girls College, Meerut University), Professor J.K. Pundir (Retired Professor of Sociology, CCS University, Meerut) and many others who have generously contributed to the Chauhan Memorial Fund.

The publication of the book would not have been possible without wholehearted support of Shri Kailash Rawat and Pranit Rawat of Rawat Publications, Jaipur. They published the book in record time. I wish to record our appreciation to Rawat Publications.

Last but not the least, thanks are due also to all those who have helped directly or indirectly in getting the book published and thereby keeping the memories of Professor B.R. Chauhan alive. Needless to say, that the Institute staff gladly collaborated in the successful completion of the project. They deserve our grateful thanks.

The Institute acknowledges Professor Chauhan's inspiring guidance and registers its appreciation for choosing the Institute as his research base. The Institute is also grateful to the ICSSR for granting this project and allowing the Institute to host it.

3 November 2017

(8th Death Anniversary of
Professor B.R. Chauhan)

T.M. Dak

Director
Institute of Social Development
Udaipur

Prolegomenon

Yogesh Atal

I am feeling somewhat uneasy writing this piece. The author of this monograph was my teacher who initiated me to the domain of sociology-anthropology. Since he is no more, the onus fell on me to prepare the press copy of his last monograph based on field work that he carried out at that advanced age, although with a team.

I recall the time when his proposal for carrying out the restudy of the village that he studied for his Ph.D., back in the 1950s, came before the ICSSR Council for financial support. As members of the Council both Professor Abha Avasthi and I pleaded in favour of the proposal, and recommended that the age bar in this case may be ignored.

We knew that he was unwell, but was keen to carry out field research himself. All kudos to him for completing the assignment despite his failing health. He left for the heavenly abode soon after submitting the dissertation to the ICSSR.

For long Professor Chauhan advocated the need to restudy the villages that were studied in the 1950s by noted scholars. When I was the Director at the ICSSR in the 1970s the Council gave restudies a priority. But none came forward. In fact, support was given for the restudy of Professor Dube's Andhra Village of Shamirpet, but nothing substantial emerged. The agenda of restudies remained on paper. The present book is the only exception, as far as I know, and hence deserves commendation. Given his age and infirmity what he did is ample proof of his commitment to social sciences.

It is for record that Professor Chauhan was the only sociologist who took his students to visit almost all the villages on which books were published in the 1950s. This was his way of teaching. He firmly believed that no amount of classroom teaching is enough for a sociology graduate if he had not done field work himself. For him, visits to these villages were like pilgrims, paying regards to the scholars who studied them. The visits also brought home the point that living societies are not static. All the villages now look different than what their descriptions tell. The element of change has a special place in sociological research. He used to quote the example of Professor Dube who came out in 1955 with his book titled *Indian Village* and then in 1958, his second book came with the title *India's Changing Villages.*

Professor Chauhan proudly said that he was able to visit so many villages that were studied in the 1950s. However, he expressed his disappointment for not being able to go to Dewas, near Indore, where our common friend, Adrian C. Mayer, had done his field work. In view of his failing health, I tried to dissuade him from going to that village. But it was in vain. Upon shifting from Bhopal to Udaipur, where he breathed his last, he phoned me to tell that he has fulfilled his wish and visited the village near Dewas while returning to Udaipur.

I bow my head to him for such dedication to work.

It is after that visit to Dewas that he engaged himself fully in completing field work with a team of researchers, and began writing the monograph on his revisit to the village of Ranawaton-ki-Sadri, where he did his first field work back in the 1950s. That monograph, titled *A Rajasthan Village* was published in 1967; a year later, my Ph.D. thesis was also published. Both these books were well received and had gone for their second editions.

Professor Chauhan was the first appointee in the State of Rajasthan to teach the newly introduced subject of Sociology at the B.A. level. Udaipur was the venue for this inaugural. At that time, Rajasthan University was mainly an examining body with the exception of teaching departments in Law and Economics in Jaipur, and Geology in Udaipur. Initially appointed as a Lecturer in Economics, Professor Chauhan was given the charge of the newly created department of Sociology at the M.B. College.

It is a tragedy that when the University of Rajasthan started Sociology Department he was denied a position there on the ground that he did not have a degree in Sociology. His juniors from the Lucknow School were taken instead. This incident encouraged him to move back to Uttar Pradesh – Agra, and later Meerut. Rajasthan lost the pioneer and an excellent teacher; Chauhan paid back his debt to his mother state of Uttar Pradesh.

Incidentally, I also did not come back to Rajasthan after I left for my M.A. to Saugar. In 1972, I was offered Professorship at Jodhpur but at that time I was already a Director in the grade of senior professor at the newly created Indian Council of Social Science Research. At the time when the appointment letter came from Jodhpur – where I was not an applicant – I was preparing for a visit to London to deliver the Prestigious Mahatma Gandhi Memorial Lecture at the University of London. The then Member-Secretary of the ICSSR took steps to retain me with him. Soon after, I was invited by UNESCO to be its First Regional Advisor for Social and Human Sciences for the vast Asia-Pacific region. It had been my privilege that I was able to associate Professor Chauhan in some major projects of UNESCO.

I, too, call myself as an ostracised social scientist from my home state. It was, therefore, strange when the professional Sociological Association of Rajasthan invited me to honour at its 2016 annual meet in Udaipur. Since this honour was given earlier to many junior, and lesser known entities, I first declined. Later, I was prevailed upon to accept it as a special honour. But at the ceremony, I felt hurt that there was no honourable mention of the contributions of Professor Chauhan; not even his photograph was displayed.

It was at this ceremony that my old classmate, Dr T.M. Dak, came to greet me. He was also sad at the neglect of our teacher. During our parley, he showed me a copy of Professor Chauhan's monograph based on the restudy of *Ranawaton-ki-Sadri* and asked me to work on it for publication. I regarded this offer as a good opportunity to pay my tribute and pay back the debt to the Guru – ऋषि ऋण. I instantly agreed.

This book, titled by him as *Restudying a Rajasthan Village*, is a posthumous publication. He completed the monograph when he was severely ill and had returned to

Udaipur as if to spend his last days in the city of his adoption. But he used his final sojourn to complete the study.

It is after his retirement that Professor Chauhan returned to his main interest in village studies. He was given a Fellowship to work on the project by the G.B. Pant Institute of Social Sciences. After completion of that project, he returned to Udaipur to begin his work on the revisit to the Village of Ranawaton-ki-Sadri, where he initially did his field work in the 1950s for his Ph.D. A liberal grant from the ICSSR helped him constitute a team of researchers to work under his guidance on the project. Not only did he ask his team to stay in the village, he himself spent considerable time there. He served as a narrator of the village of yore and asked his team to locate the key differences in the village between 1950s and the first decade of the 21st century.

As a field anthropologist, he insisted on observation and informal interviews. But he allowed the team to consult the enormous secondary data relative to the village and the region to locate changes occurring in the village as a consequence of urbanization and modernization, democratic decentralization, and the emerging party politics.

The author has restrained from making sweeping generalizations and focussed on the changes at the microcosmic level, relating them to the changing socio-politico climate of the country as a whole.

While Chauhan was keen on injecting a historical dimension, the limitation of time and the paucity of historical data regarding the village, prevented him to pursue that approach. The study, therefore, turned out to be a synchronic study. Wherever possible, he provided secondary data mainly from the government documents that was a substitute for the historical dimension. Some other data were culled out from the memories of his old respondents, and from the examples of changed structures since the first study.

Having studied the same village at two points of time Chauhan had the advantage of deciphering change, in the format: T2-T1=C. Certainly T2 is the changed state from T1 when the village was studied first. Case studies of some new institutions and physical structures can be treated as additions to the village structure. Noticing changes in the performance of religious rituals can be regarded as examples of new equations of continuity and change.

The style of narration is unique. Through his memory lane, the author has moved from one street to another recording the transformations and continuities. He found that people continue to adhere to certain traditions, particularly in interpreting calamities as the wrath of visiting deities; however, they also are not averse to accept the modern cure. Modernization is not a replacement of tradition. It is a new equation of accommodation of tradition and modernity. He also hinted that some traditional ways, particularly among the lower castes, are closer to the modernity and need not be erased; in fact, they need to be introduced among the so-called upper castes.

Chauhan found that some members of the occupational castes in the village population are moving to other vocations in the modern economic sector, while others are practising their traditional vocation. In fact, the artisan castes have found advantage in continuing their traditional occupation not only in the urban areas of the country – within Mewar or other neighbouring States (such as Gujarat and Maharashtra) – but even in the countries of the Gulf. In fact, they prefer to work in the caste-related vocations like carpentry and iron smithy; rather than moving over to other vocations. Thus, continuity of traditional caste-related occupations in the case of the young people is not forced on them by other so-called superior castes. In a similar fashion, people make their own choices in giving up caste-related menial jobs. No other caste forces them to stick to their traditional jobs or to do chores they did not like. This falsifies the prevailing notion of exploitation of lower castes, at least in the changing milieu.

For example, in the 1950s, villages such as Ranawaton-ki-Sadri did not have old fashioned family toilets requiring someone to remove the night soil. People went in open for answering their natural calls. Now with the introduction of pipelines, and the electricity, houses are building toilets that have the facility of the flush. Removal of the night soil was an urban necessity, and it was the low grade vocation. It is in the urban centres, and not in the villages, that such evil practice prevailed. There is also the toilet revolution, as part of the Swachchhata Abhiyan (स्वच्छता अभियान), run by the Modi government. It is gradually erasing this stigma, and must be emphasised.

The village literacy profile is changing rapidly, particularly among the younger age group. There are even encouraging signs of the spread of literacy among girls. The village now has a school for girls, *pucca* roads can take senior students, using a bicycle, to neighbouring large villages for higher studies. The Panchayats, under the

Programme of Democratic Decentralization, have opened the doors for the village women to partake in village decision-making.

The book is written in a descriptive style as ethnography of a changing village. At several places, Chauhan has hinted at the prospects for further chiselling. There are references to other theoreticians giving tips to the reader to elaborate those points further.

Since this work was carried out by a team of researchers, it lacks a certain unity and the flow that one finds in his 1967 study. As the very first attempt to restudy the same society, this book, however, is special.

Let me hope that some of his young students will carry the flame further and fulfil his dream of revisiting the old and famous research sites that provided rich empirical data to understand contemporary India, rather than quoting all the time someone who became famous as Manu. Empirical studies of the villages and of caste carried out since 1950s did not repeat Manu, but provided more authentic field data to understand social structure of contemporary India.

Yogesh Atal

The Author and the Editor

Mutual Introductions

Since this book is a queer amalgam of author's version and editing done posthumously, it will be useful to have as a PRELUDE introductions of both, the author and the editor. For this novel method, we found an essay written by the editor on the author and vice versa. Both are produced in this section.

Yogesh Atal introducing Brij Raj Chauhan

1 March 1927 – 3 November 2009

Coming from a small village, Chak-Salempur, in Etawah District of Western Uttar Pradesh, Chauhan's father, Shri Ran Bahadur Sinha,[1] was brought to Udaipur as Head Master of the Bhopal Nobles' School. This was an elite school where children of the feudal families of Mewar were sent for education. Child Brij Raj also received his early education at the same school. Both he, and his elder brother,

Prithvi Raj, were sent to Agra and then to Lucknow for their higher education. Brij Raj did his intermediate from the Balwant Rajput College, Agra, and then went to Lucknow University to do B.A. (honours) and M.A. in Economics (with specialization in Sociology). He then enrolled himself for the LL.B. degree and chose the Hindi medium for answering question papers.

Udaipur of those days – in the 1930s and 40s – was a small township of around 30,000 people; even though it was the capital of the princely state of Mewar. The local population had a few persons with college degrees, such as BA, obtained from outside of Mewar, mainly from the United Provinces.[2] Even high schools were affiliated to Agra University, which conducted the examinations. In such circumstances, arrival of Chauhan's father as School Head Master was a big happening for Udaipur, and the family earned all the respect and adoration from the locals. As Head Master of the Bhopal Nobles' School, and later as its Principal, when the School was upgraded to become a College, his father belonged to the select group of academic elite in the town, and was held in high esteem. He finally settled in the new colony of Bhopalpura, on the outskirts of the walled city. Since Professor Chauhan left Udaipur, in the mid-1960s, to teach at Agra Institute of Social Sciences, and then at the Meerut University, his parents went back to Etawah.

Chauhan's return to Udaipur, after his post-graduation, happily coincided with the opening of Sociology department in the College. When the post of the Lecturer was advertised for the newly created Department, the lawyer-in-the making chose to apply for it. And he got selected. Thus began his career in Sociology in September

1949, and thus began the teaching of Sociology in Rajasthan – M.B. College was then the only College in the entire state of Rajasthan to offer Sociology at the B.A. level. Because of his degree – as M.A. in Economics – he was asked to share some teaching in Economics and, in addition teach the papers on Sociology and Social Psychology to the students of Political Science. He used that opportunity to inject sociological perspective in the disciplines of economics and political science. In fact, in economics, he initiated the teaching of Planning and Development, and encouraged economics students to undertake field research for their Masteral dissertation.

A young graduate from Lucknow, clad in khadi clothes, fluent in English and Hindi, teaching three subjects – economics, political science, and sociology, and a cricket player who had the record of making a century in the Ranji trophy tournament – Professor Chauhan[3] became an object of veneration in the college and the city. He had scholarly looks, and his commitment to *Khadi*[4] earned him the prestige of being a patriot and a "Gandhian". It was shirt and trouser, or Kurta-Pyjama in summer, and a Sherwani or *Bandgala* jacket in winter that would identify him. After the classes, he could be seen at the College playground coaching the budding cricketers. And while returning home, he was always accompanied by a small group of students – either cricket players or bookworm students, or both – riding on bicycles and engaged in conversations with him. In fact, these journeys were the "functional equivalent" of "tutorials" in which Professor Chauhan conducted his extra-mural dialogues. Invariably the short trips from the College to the outskirts of the city ended with a sitting session in a tea-stall, the teacher always playing the host. The informal togetherness did not, however, disturb the teacher-taught role set. These were occasions for the students to come closer to the "intellectual giant", to get free tuition, and get moulded in academic culture. Professor Chauhan chose to be the students' teacher, unlike others who maintained reasonable distance from the students. He also promoted social work – not the subject, but the selfless work for the cause of society. The staircase at the College playing ground for game watchers, and a huge open air theatre in the college compound was constructed through voluntary participation of the students that he organised. This manner of labour donation later came to be known as *Shram Daan* (श्रम दान).

Obliquely trained as a sociologist, and teaching sociology not only to the undergraduate students, but also to students doing their M.A. in Political Science[5], Chauhan sharpened his sociological imagination by treating his social interactions as laboratory experiments. He was the lone sociology teacher in the College. There was no immediate superior in the College, or in the town, to guide him. Obviously, there were several topics that he was also reading for the first time, and with a view to teaching them. With the wisdom of the hindsight, I can now say that his interactions with students outside of the classroom were part of a mutual learning experience. The concepts discussed in the classroom were brought in extra mural conversations and efforts were made to find suitable illustrations. Primary group, nuclear family, prestige and esteem, status and role, function – and countless other concepts – were tried to be understood through walk-and-talk sessions on the streets of Udaipur and through visits to the nearby villages. Professor Chauhan and the small group of students that got "attached" to him were getting socialized in the culture of sociology, and learning its vocabulary through such sessions.

While Uttar Pradesh was flooded with cheap and unreliable textbooks – written in Hindi by ill-informed writers – Udaipur was then relatively untouched. A small class of 40–50 persons was not an attractive market for the publishers of cheap textbooks. The students of sociology at Udaipur were *per force* made to read *Society* by MacIver and Page and *Cultural Sociology* by Gillin and Gillin. Professor Chauhan based his lectures on these two sources, and ingeniously explicated the key concepts with Indian examples drawn from day-to-day social life. Since most students – including myself – took the examinations through the Hindi medium, it became necessary for the teacher to lecture first in English and then offer a detailed Hindi summary in the last lecture on a given topic. For several individual topics, students were made to read from the standard books in English. The fact that Professor Chauhan was teaching only at the B.A. level, he set high standards matching the expectations of M.A.

I came in his contact in 1953 when I joined the College as a student of F.A. – what is now called Intermediate. Since sociology was taught only at the B.A. level, I had no opportunity to witness his class, and to come in his direct contact. My first encounter with him was when he was one of the judges for an elocution contest – called debate competition – in the College. The contestants were from all the classes, including M.A. final. I was the junior most, from first year of the intermediate class. Since I came first in that competition, I earned a place in Professor Chauhan's inner circle of students. After the debate, I was invited to join his group on the bicycles to return to the town, and got the opportunity to spend time in a restaurant, sipping tea with him. He used that occasion to analyse my performance in the debate competition and to indicate the strong and weak points, in the most constructive manner. That was the beginning of our interaction which continued till he breathed his last. I was informed of his death at midnight. I took the first available flight to reach Udaipur for the funeral rites.

Walking aimlessly, and for longer hours, every day on the streets of Udaipur in the company of Professor Chauhan, and his inner circle, I got my first lessons in sociology. With that orientation, it was not a difficult decision for me to opt for sociology as one of the electives in B.A.; Hindi and Economics were the other optionals. And I chose the Hindi medium; the only English I learnt was through the compulsory paper.

When I joined the B.A. class, Professor Chauhan gave me a gift packet. It was a newly purchased copy of MacIver and Page's *Society.* Judging by the standard of those days, it was a costly book of Rs 20. The gift not only spoke of the great generosity of the teacher, but also conveyed his expectations from me. Of course, I was not alone to earn such a favour. There were some others also who were similarly rewarded in previous years. At a time when the salary of a lecturer was around Rs 150 per month, spending so much on students was not an ordinary matter. It was, therefore, a distinct honour for me, and also a constant reminder that I must not frustrate the teacher by my poor performance at the examinations. I still hold that book as my treasure. Since I had that book, I read it all even as a B.A. student with poor command of the English language then, and knowing fully well that I will have to translate the ideas into Hindi to answer the questions. This is how he kept us away from cheap cook books, and made our foundations strong.

The money for such donations came from an unusual source. Every year, college teachers were engaged in invigilation duties during the university examinations. Professor Chauhan used the payments received for such extra work for buying the books to gift the deserving and needy students. In my case, it was a little more than this. When he despatched me to Sagar to do my M.A., he sent to Professor Dube the entire invigilation fee he received for that year with the request that it should be given to me if I were in financial difficulty, but not letting me know the source of that bounty. It can be well imagined how I must have felt when I learnt of this from Professor Dube much later. Certainly, this act earned him great respect in the eyes of Professor Dube; and the hidden message about my penury conveyed to him brought me closer to my mentor. I became Professor Dube's adopted son. On my passing out, Professor Dube gifted me his costly Omega watch. I was also recruited in a research project even prior to the declaration of the result. The money that Professor Chauhan sent to professor Dube for my use was then donated to other needy students for paying their fee or buying a book.

Professor Chauhan used other extramural ways to teach sociology to us. He always insisted that society is the laboratory for the sociologists and that, unlike the physical sciences where the researchers can create experimental conditions, sociologists are required to understand the events when they occur, in their natural settings. He himself chose to work for his doctorate in social anthropology, and that too in a village – not in the tribal setting, which was, and still is, the forte of anthropology. It is in that spirit that he went back to the village which he studied in the 1950s to see how much has changed and what kind of reorientation is needed for the students doing village studies.

In the early hours of the 3 November 2009, Professor Brij Raj Chauhan, aged 82 years 8 months, breathed his last in Udaipur, Rajasthan. It is this city where he spent his childhood as part of the family that migrated from a small village in western Uttar Pradesh, and where he returned after graduation from Lucknow to be the first lecturer in sociology in the state of Rajasthan in the year 1949. After his stints at Agra Institute of Social Sciences and at the Meerut University, he finally returned to Udaipur to resume his work and to retire. Udaipur became his exit door.

Professor Chauhan is author of several articles and books both in English and Hindi. His publications include *A Rajasthan Village* (1967 and 1999); *Towns in the Tribal Setting* (1970); *Scheduled Castes and Education* (1975); *Bharat Mein Grameen Samaj (भारत में ग्रामीण समाज)* (1988); *India: A Socio-Economic Profile* (1989); *Rural-Urban Articulations* (1991); and *Samaj Vigyan Ke Prerak Srot (समाज विज्ञान के प्रेरक स्त्रोत) (1994)*.

Notes

1. The last name is pronounced as *Simh*, meaning lion. All Rajputs in Mewar have the same name ending, but in English they write *Singh* so as not to confuse with *Sinha* (pronounced as Sin haa), used by the Kayastha caste, mainly

in Eastern Uttar Pradesh and Bihar. It is interesting that while the father did not use the caste or clan name, his sons suffixed their names with *Chauhan*; this may have been prompted by the culture of the Nobles' School where everybody used the clan name as a suffix to the personal name. His sons suffixed their names with *Chauhan*.

2. Which later was renamed Uttar Pradesh, thus retaining the acronym UP.
3. All the teachers in the College were then addressed as "Professor" irrespective of their official designation as lecturer or Head of the Department; those who got their doctorate had the honour of being addressed as "Doctor". Thus, doctor was regarded as a superior position. The colleges did not follow the University hierarchy of lecturer, reader, and professor. For the common man, a teacher in the school was a "Master Sahib" and a college teacher as "Professor Sahib". This was a good example of the distinction between *private* and *public* status, made in sociology textbooks.
4. He wore khadi all his life. However, he had a suit bought in 1961 when he went to the USA for further studies; occasionally, he wore that suit. He had a tie but needed someone to tie the knot.
5. He taught to them two papers, one on Contemporary Sociological Theories, and the other on Social Psychology, using the books authored by Pitirim Sorokin and Mc Dougall.

Chauhan introducing Atal[1]

[condensed version by T.M. Dak]

Yogesh Atal:
Born 9 October 1937

Yogesh Atal caught my attention when he joined Maharana Bhopal College as a student of intermediate class and participated and won debates competing with students from higher classes. His performance at the BA level in various tests and presentations distinguished himself from the rest; he participated in field trips, wrote small papers, and presented a paper to the first Rajasthan Sociological Conference we had organized at the Maharana Bhopal College, Udaipur in 1955 when Yogesh was in the first year of B.A. The late Professors K.M. Kapadia (who presided over the Conference) and I.P. Desai lent grace to the Conference, and commended Yogesh for his presentation.

Yogesh Atal's interests and inclinations for the subject began by going through the reading of *Society* by MacIver and Page and *Indian Village* authored by Professor S.C. Dube. With performance in the examinations at the top level, he was sure to get admission in the newly opened M.A. classes in Sociology in Udaipur itself. But I advised him to go to Sagar and study with S.C. Dube. That was a difficult decision. I had to convince his grandfather of the difference it would make.

Dube exercised great influence on the younger talented minds of India at that time, and encouraged them to feel confident. As an excellent teacher with competence in the latest trends in the subject, and an avid reader of books till 2 am at home, he cast a spell over his students. Additionally, Sagar was a place where a small group of teachers – hardly half a dozen – frequently met to discuss the complex philosophical issues, which used to be neatly summarized by Daya Krishna of the Philosophy Department. Dube had a unique sense of feeling the pulse of emerging questions in sociology in the world at large and their relevance for India. He guided the students along those channels thereby encouraging and equipping them to work in the advanced fields. Some of them could seize the opportunity and acquire self-confidence. Yogesh Atal was one of them; Dube showed his interest in Hindi literature – he was a known Hindi writer – and this brought young Yogesh Atal into still more empathic touch with him, a relationship that continued all through Dube's life and even after.

The youngster, Yogesh Atal, became an effective teacher in Chandigarh and Agra. Later, he moved to the Indian Institute of Technology, Delhi. The latter assignment gave him an opportunity to introduce newer subjects in the traditional curricula; he introduced teaching of Management, newer processes of social and culture change, and the then emerging concept of Modernization. He was the first one among the Indian sociologists to work on election studies and political behaviour. He also anchored many TV programmes when this medium was limited only to the mega cities.

Yogesh's visit to the United States in 1964 on a Smith-Mundt Fellowship and a Fulbright Travel Grant added to his capacity for undertaking exercises in collating and interpreting secondary data and planning for researches "beyond the village". His association with Paul Lazarsfeld and Robert K. Merton made him an interesting learner in the process of research in which an empirical expert joined issues with a theoretician.

This made it possible for Atal to plan an inquiry into the *Local Communities and National Politics*[2], which in point of time marked a systematic effort in the growing area of Political Sociology as well as Election Studies in India. It also marked the stage whereby a trained social anthropologist acquired sociological sophistication in the choice of the theme, linking the local with the state and the national scene, and introducing panel studies as technique of social research at the operational level in India. He was actively engaged in macro-level studies in India on the (i) perception of national threat during the Chinese invasion, (ii) a series of election studies covering various states of the country, and (iii) study of educational problems of the children of Scheduled Castes and Scheduled Tribes.

From Merton, more specifically, Yogesh drew a new source of inspiration as a teacher who would take a newspaper cutting for the day, and go on explaining the nuances of sociological formulations through it, the manner in which history of ideas and science could be traced to seventeenth and eighteenth century sources, and the ever continuing interest in classics, with Merton feeling the need to have one more look into Durkheim's works, besides the concepts like *functions* and *dysfunctions* – manifest and latent – that effortlessly became a part of the vocabulary. Yogesh Atal's article on "Managing Multiplicity" (published in the *Economic and Political Weekly* of 9 September 2001) received personal notice of Merton who complimented him for taking a significant step in the extension of the formulations on *Insiders and Outsiders* to a situation like the one in India.

Beyond the academic arena, Yogesh Atal conducted himself with dignity as a Director at the Indian Council of Social Science Research (ICSSR) from where he graduated to become UNESCO's Regional Adviser for Social and Human Sciences in Asia and the Pacific, and then working at the headquarters in Paris as Principal Director of Social Sciences till his retirement in 1997. His last assignment at UNESCO was Coordinator of UNESCO for the World Social Summit which was held in 1995 in Copenhagen, Denmark.

The tenure with the ICSSR brought him under the guidance of an able administrator of the quality of J.P. Naik, who was well known for his dexterity in dealing with the files, his grip over details, particularly in the educational field, and his acceptability by the greats in social sciences and administration. At short notice, J.P. Naik could produce documented texts for important addresses to be delivered by the cabinet minister. Yogesh Atal imbibed quite a few of these qualities, yet assiduously kept himself away from the simple Gandhian style of life that had become a hallmark of J.P. Naik's personality. What mattered, however, was the work culture. The placement in the ICSSR also meant increased meaningful relations with the prominent social scientists, philosophers, and historians of the country. A seminar organized at the Indian Institute of Advanced Study, Shimla, brought scholars from Asian region together, creating the climate for an initiative for Asia. The word reached UNESCO headquarters in Paris where the idea of the Asian Regional Office was mooted and the young Atal who had delivered the goods in practice was picked up for the position of its Director, of course after due advertisement and recruitment process. A stint of training in the French language, and then training in the UNESCO Culture of Work made Yogesh an effective administrator in the UN System.

Success at an early age made Yogesh Atal a talking point in drawing room conversations amongst professionals. As UNESCO Adviser for Asia and the Pacific, Yogesh Atal helped social science organizations of different countries of the region, establishing relations with such social scientists as mattered cutting across disciplines. He could pick up a political scientist from the Philippines where he had a significant role to assume in the country's polity, could observe the recycling process of irrigation and electricity generation in North Korea, besides getting entry into China and Pakistan through his diplomatic passport, thereby informing himself of the areas hitherto not familiar to the Indian social scientists. I was happy to learn from the Vice Chancellor of the New England University in Australia of his understanding of a UNESCO official in the person of Yogesh Atal, a relationship he mentioned to clinch support for a proposal mooted at a seminar in Sydney. And this was in the absence of Atal. While doing a stock taking of Asian Social Science, Yogesh Atal hit the nail on the head when he said, "Asian social scientists are geographically proximate and culturally close, but they are academically remote from each other". Even the limited access was through the Western scholarship both in ideas and methods. This made him rethink on the need for *indigenization* of social sciences, a theme on which the Asian social scientists concentrated their attention, his Paper providing the impetus. It is largely through his effective interventions at the international level that the significance of national sociologies is now being discussed, and we are asked to provide a sort of justification for being 'Indians' in terms of our concerns and approaches that could be our trade mark. It is one of the ironies of circumstances that the initial sustained work put into this debate by a social scientist working through an international agency has yet to be noticed in this country, leave aside recognized.

Beyond the Asia-Pacific region, Yogesh Atal conducted seminars on rural-urban articulations, and the papers prepared for such discussions were published in the *International Social Science Journal* (UNESCO, Paris), and reproduced in several languages.

Atal retired from UNESCO after playing a major role as UNESCO's Coordinator for the World Summit for Social Development held in Copenhagen in March 1995. As a follow-up to the Summit, he encouraged a series of studies on Poverty in the former Socialist block, and came out with the very first publication under the title *Poverty in Transition and Transition in Poverty.* This book is a standard reference in many universities in the United States.

On retirement he has begun to serialize his experiences for various publications. He returned to his pet theme in Political Sociology and researched the 1999 elections in India that brought back Vajpayee to power.

That book, titled *Mandate for Political Transition*, compares the manifestoes of contending political parties, essays the success of the BJP and its alliances and cautions them on dangers of over-enthusiasm in certain directions. This is once again a work on macro dimension in India with newspapers providing data, but the author insists, during my conversations with him, that anthropological insights pervade his interpretations, a claim that I would not accede to with the felicity with which it is offered. With a computer at hand, Yogesh Atal sets and resets his contributions to provide timely pieces for publication in areas where he thinks social scientists have the capacity to work, but are somehow shying away from making timely interventions.

I may now specify a few of the areas where his hard serious work could have received greater recognition. His analysis of group alliances cutting across castes in a village, and the application of a theoretical construct of *basic* or *pivotal*, *sufficiently relevant*, and *peripheral* attributes to the nature of caste as a unit and a system, that figures in his work on *The Changing Frontiers of Caste, comes* in that category. The link between the rural, town, and urban Centre to see the impact of communication on election choices, and his use of the panel technique for the first time in Indian sociology for election studies are significant in his second work titled *Local Communities and National Politics.* His paper on "The Call for Indigenization" deserves to be noted. Expanding the frontiers of sociology to nations as units and the relevance of the Asia-Pacific region, as also the exercises to research issues relative to development and poverty are other contributions of Atal that deserve to be acknowledged.

Notes

1. Taken from *Emerging Social Science Concerns* edited by Surendra Gupta (2004). The volume was devoted to felicitate Professor Yogesh Atal, and was published by Concept Publication, New Delhi.
2. Published by National Publishing House, 1971.

The Book:
Indian Village Revisited

Preface

This is a report of the revisit to the village in the Mewar area of Rajasthan that the author had intensively studied for the first time in 1955. The book, which is based on this field research conducted erased and titled *Rajasthan Village*, was first published in 1967. In the second edition of the book, 30 years later in 1999, the author highlighted some of the changes that have occurred in the village's social structure. He then felt the need for a restudy of the village; in fact, he felt convinced that all the Indian villages that have been studied in the 1950s by sociologists and anthropologists ought to be restudied to gauge the changes they have been experiencing as a consequence of large-scale planned social change initiated by the government of independent India.

This short report is based on the revisit to the village after a lapse of nearly 50 years. However, it is not a study of the village at two points of time. It attempts to document the process through which structural arrangements and rearrangements have occurred in the community and other practices still prevalent in region which indicate continuity in the midst of changes.

The author has carried the time frame of enquiry farther back than the initial study with a view to looking into points of diversification of the main clan of the *Ranawat* who inhabited the village. The village was first inhabited by Viram Dev who belonged to the Ranawat clan that is linked to Maharana Pratap's second son, Amar Singh. This group is said to have been separated from Shaktawat clan whose originator was Shakti Singh, younger brother of legendary Maharana Pratap. The differences between Maharana Pratap and Shakti Singh were so great that the latter virtually broke all ties and allied with Mughal Emperor Akbar and fought against him; however, he finally returned to Pratap's camp when the Mughal army virtually overpowered Pratap and his favourite horse *Chetak* was mortally attacked.

Ranawats of the village under study trace their lineage through the nearby village of Sanwad. The team visited this village also to fill in certain gaps in genealogy.

The Indian Council of Social Science Research financed the project. By far, this is the only restudy of an Indian village.

It must be recorded here that in the interim the author has paid visits to the villages that have been earlier studied by pioneers in rural research in India. He took some of his students to several villages, including those that have been studied earlier, for an exposure to village life as part of the training in rural sociology. These visits also covered the two villages in the Saharanpur District that S.C. Dube studied to gauge the changes that have occurred due to the introduction of the Community Development Programme in India. These villages became regular sites for visits for the students of the Meerut University's Department of Sociology. Incidentally, Dube's book, *India's Changing Villages* (Routledge and

Kegan Paul, 1958), was the first to dwell on the impact of community development initiatives over the village life with specific focus on cultural changes in the village. It was used for the training of sociology students and also senior-level officers in the Indian Administrative Service.

The author organised study courses of smaller duration in the two villages studied by S.C. Dube. Such exercises became a part of teaching and research in sociology at the University of Meerut where the author worked as Professor and Head of the Department.

The author's 1990 publication, *Rural-Urban Articulations* (1990), was based on field work conducted in three villages of this region, of which one was part of Dube's study. During field work, half-a-dozen scholars from the USA came to visit the site and to conduct field studies in the chosen villages. Constant interaction and discussion with these scholars was indeed very enriching. In addition, the author took his students to other villages that have been studied in the 1950s and the books based on field research in them became major landmarks in Indian sociology. These visits took the Meerut Team to Shamirpet studied by S.C. Dube, and published by Routledge and Kegan Paul, London (1955)[1]; Sripuram, a Tanjore Village studied by Andre Beteille (1965); three villages in Uttar Pradesh, including Mohana near Lucknow, were studied by D.N. Majumdar's team (1958); Kishan Garhi, near Aligarh, was studied by McKim Marriott (1955); Sherupur was studied by Harold Gould (1987); and a Gujarat village named Vedchi was studied by I.P. Desai (1977). The author had also paid a visit in 2003 to Rampura, a village near Mysore which was studied by M.N. Srinivas (1955), and the village Awan in Kota District in Rajasthan, which was studied by Giri Raj Gupta (1974). One of the villages where Yogesh Atal conducted field studies for his book, *The Changing Frontiers of Caste* (1968), is located within 30 kilometres of Ranawaton-ki-Sadri – the village under restudy; the study team visited that village in 2004. The author also visited the village near Dewas, Indore, which was studied by Adrian C. Mayer.[2]

While carrying out the village study in Rajasthan, it became clear that the village was part of a wider social network. It was not an isolated unit. This was also the experience of other scholars doing fieldwork in the villages in the 1950s. The villagers had meaningful interactions with neighbouring villages and towns, and their social life cannot be understood without acknowledging this facet of their life.

It is for this reason that while in the original study we focussed on the single village, treating it as a *unity*, and in the present restudy we have paid equal attention to its extensions by covering about ten more villages in its neighbourhood.

The origin of the Ranawat clan has been traced to six further ascending generations through reliable records. Their arrival in the village and multiplication of the families in the village brought into operation two more social units, that is, the compound family (first mentioned by Leach in the study *Pul Eliya*, 1954) and disconnected families, into some sort of neighbourhoods. These are presented in Chapter 3 of this book. The rural base and its connections with other villages and towns have been presented for each caste separately in Chapter 4. The organisation of ritual life in the village has been viewed for its communitarian character via two festivals; these are reported in Chapter 5. This study also covered the events connected with major life events such as marriage, remarriage and death.

The extension of state-sponsored activities and institutions, particularly those of the Panchayati Raj, added a fresh dimension to rural life. These are covered in Chapter 6. Inter-village relationships become important when the area of a Gram Panchayat and the constituency of electing a member to the Panchayat Samiti at the block level are required to cover a population of more than 5,000. For us, this meant coverage of five rural settlements. This helped us work out inter-village and inter-caste configurations in the extended area. The local-level politics acquires greater dynamism when special treatment is meted out to people belonging to demographic groups such as Scheduled Category (SCs) and to women.

Besides summarising the main findings the concluding Chapter presents the overall perspective on longitudinal intensive studies of rural life. Historical dimensions provide the touchstone for examining whether structural elements have had continuity or have undergone changes.

The extension of the inquiry, both over time and space, necessitated the use of a variety of tools and source materials. Chapter 2 is devoted to explain the methodology used for the collection of data for the present study.

It is hoped that such a presentation will help in conducting researches in other villages through further innovative steps.

The Research Team

The first study of the Rajasthan village that began in 1955 centred on observations made by the author himself. The period of restudy in 2003–2004 is marked by a little change organisationally. This time the study was carried out by a team of researchers led by T.R. Singh[3] along with Manoj Dashora, Yogesh Kumar Raghav, and Pankaj Kumar Singh who paid several field visits to the village and the surrounding region. Arun Chauhan accompanied the team occasionally during field visits and joined the in-house discussions – a special feature of the project in which the field workers were involved even at the writing stage for verification and providing personalised inputs for the presentation.

It is with pleasure that I acknowledge the cooperation of the members of the village community who spared their time and allowed us to write about their activities and experiences. Various courtesies extended to the research team during our presence in the village are gratefully acknowledged.

The study was carried out under the auspices of the Institute of Social Development, Udaipur and was funded by the Indian Council for Social Science Research. Dr T.M. Dak, the Director of the Institute, looked after organisational matters, including tabulation and review of the first draft of the Report. Technical assistance provided by Yakub Mohammed, Chitresh Joshi, Mohd. Kadir, and Jyoti helped in the final presentation of the report. Ramesh Chandra deserves our grateful thanks for undertaking two visits to the village for videography.

The ICSSR made available a generous grant for the project via the Institute of Social Development. The author is grateful, both to the ICSSR and to ISD, for the support extended to this study. However, these agencies are in no way responsible for the contents of the report for which the author alone takes the responsibility.

5 October 2005 **Brij Raj Chauhan**

2, Darshanpura, Udaipur

Notes

1. The year 1955 was important as three major works were published on rural India. Besides Dube's *Indian Village*, two anthologies of village studies were also published, namely, *Village India* (edited by McKim Marriott), and *India's Villages* (edited by M.N. Srinivas).
2. Lessons of these visits will be written about separately, but it will suffice to mention here that the purpose was to get insight into the field work. It was heartening to note that many villagers still recall the fond memories of their interactions with these noted fieldworkers who have earned a name in the profession. The personal bond between these researchers and the residents of areas of their work has their own intimacy and confidence that can be counted as an inspiration and a treasure for the young researchers in the discipline.

   Alas! This has remained an unfulfilled agenda as the author passed away soon after completing this report and one more book, titled Rural Life: Grassroots Perspective; New Delhi, Concept Publishing Company, 2009. Professor Chauhan died on 3 November 2009.
3. T.R. Singh was associated with the initial study carried out by Dube in Saharanpur district. His assignment as teacher in a college in Roorkee was another plus point. His comparative view on field work in rural areas of Andhra Pradesh, Madhya Pradesh, Uttar Pradesh, Orissa, Maharashtra and Gujarat was indeed an asset for the project. His contribution is gratefully acknowledged.

1

Sources of Data

A Methodological Note

This is a report on the revisit to the village after a lapse of nearly 40 years. However, it is not a study of the village at two points of time. It attempts to document the process through which structural arrangements and rearrangements have occurred in the community and the region during the interregnum.

The study relates to a village situated in Mewar, near the Fateh Nagar railway station on the Udaipur–Chittorgarh railway line. The village is named *Ranawaton-ki-Sadri.* The origins of the village can be traced back to Viramdev, a historical figure who had considerable influence in the region. Viramdev's uncle Shakti Singh, younger brother of Maharana Amar Singh, created his own clan named *Shaktawat,* to part company with the descendants of Ranawats. The descendants of Maharana Pratap belonged to the Ranawat sub-clan. Maharana Pratap's lineage was the third in this kinship web.

To draw the contours of the village's physical and social structure the research team was able to procure secondary data from various governmental sources. Such information, it must be underlined, was not available when the village was first studied in the 1960s.

Secondary Data for Drawing the Village Profile

Historical Records

Among the published sources, two works are of basic significance. Around 1820s Col. James Tod, the representative of the British East India Company, took special care to compile historical records and brought out the first internationally recognised work, *The Annals and Antiquities of Rajasthan* (1999). The work has a literary flavour. The Rajputs of this region, which was then called *Rajputana*, have respect for Col. Tod 'for being the person who made' them aware for their 'historical connections'. The work has been subjected to great scrutiny by historians who felt the need to sort out parts that are descriptive of real happenings and those that are dedicated to the glorification of events.

The other source of the history of Rajput rule in Mewar is the work authored by Shyamal Das, a Minister in the Government of Mewar. The volume was titled *Veer Vinod.* Shyamal Das was granted leave of office by the Maharana to concentrate on writing this monograph. This publication is the authentic history of Mewar, including Mewar's relations with the neighbouring states and the Mughal rulers in Delhi. The account also includes the period of Maratha and the British rule in India.

In this mammoth exercise, the period of each of the ruling chiefs of Mewar, particularly Maharana Kumbha and his heirs, has been described in detail. Shyamal Das has described in detail the role played by various chieftains in different battles. It also provides detailed information about the rulers of Mewar, particularly their administrative setup, important construction works like forts and palaces, as well as lakes and gardens. The work includes references to various castes, details of princely marriages, specialties of lineages with occasional references to customs and traditions, as well as the arrival of new influences. Compiled in 20 parts, and running into 2259 pages in octavo size, this compendium ends with the demise of Maharana Sajjan Singh on 23 December 1884.

Maharana Sajjan Singh was succeeded by Maharana Fateh Singh whose tenure lasted for 46 years (1884–1930). And it was during the first three years of his rule that the work entitled *Veer Vinod* was completed, that is, 1887–1889.

The author, Shyamal Das, belonged to the caste of Charan, the panegyrists, who wrote poetry in praise of rulers and maintained genealogies of the royal clan. The Charan enjoyed immunity for their compositions; the king would pardon a poet in case of an objectionable metaphor. The work *Veer Vinod* has become the standard reference for history and culture of Mewar, despite being eulogical. It continues to be the most quoted reference for research on the region.

For the authentic history of Mewar two references are most quoted: Gauri Shankar Hira Chand Ojha's *Udaipur Rajya ka Itihas* (1927), and Gopi Nath Sharma's *Mewar during the Mughals.* Gopi Nath Sharma's subsequent work on social and cultural life of Mewar is also a useful reference.

The first edition of *A Rajasthan Village* (Chauhan, 1967) made use of the above-mentioned works. G.N. Sharma, a colleague at the M.B. College, went through the manuscript of my book and made useful comments.

Lineage Charts and Thikana Records

The Rajput heads of the villages, such as the village understudy, maintained some sort of *Thikana* records. The most important part is record related to the point from which their ancestors branched off from the royal family. Each successive occupants of the seat of the power, *Thikana*, is mentioned in these papers. In case of Sanwad, the records relate to 14 successors of the young prince Viramdev, the third son of Maharana Udai Singh who had ascended the throne of Mewar in 1537AD.

The kingdom followed the rule of primogeniture in succession; childless kings adopted a child of near kin who became the inheritor of the kingdom. Younger brothers of the king were donated villages away from the main Thikana – seat of power. The revenue earned from these villages went to these *Jagirdars* (landlords). For ready reference, they maintained the list of all the Maharanas of the state of Mewar, including the period of their rule. In later records information is also given about the invading Muslim rulers occupying the seat of the Emperor in Delhi. That list begins with the rule of Mahmud Ghaznawi.

Our team obtained copies of these records, courtesy of the current descendant of the branch of Sanwad Thikana. These documents enabled us to locate the villages in which the Viramdev branch is currently spread. Ranawaton-ki-Sadri bifurcated from Sanwad some six generations ago. There is detailed description of the conditions under which the owners of the village understudy got separated from their parent lineage. In the 1965 study, links of the family with the founder of two lineages were not recorded.[1] The availability of such material opens possibilities of adding historical dimensions to sociological inquiries depending on the manner in which sociologists make use of the material, particularly dealing with the social situation in princely states.

Records at the District and the Panchayat Samiti Offices

At the village level, a number of new records are now available because of the new development schemes initiated by the government. These can be found at the offices of the Panchayat Samiti, Revenue Circles and the Village Panchayat and at some other official units functioning at the village level. One is reminded of the manner in which William Beveridge had faced the problem of paucity of data before launching schemes of social security immediately after the Second World War. In his times, data were generated with the implementation of the scheme.

The nature of such data and the type of information they contain may now be summarised.

Zila Sankhyikiya Roop Rekha – 2001, Chittorgarh

The district statistical outline, published by the Economic and Statistics Directorate, Jaipur, contains classified information under 22 heads dealing with various departments. It begins with the general information at the administrative level, then goes on to cover data in area and population composition. Information classified along Panchayat Samiti levels helps locate the general characteristics on various items. The broader picture of the Panchayat Samiti provides a view of the area within which a particular village is located. In turn, conclusions of single-village studies are placed within a sub-regional space, which paves way for making valid generalizations at the sub-regional level. The data are a valuable source for defining the broad contours of the village community. However, they need to be processed in a manner as to obtain sociologically significant inferences.

The data pertaining to the *Tehsil* of rural Kapasan indicate a respectable sex ratio: 975 females per 1,000 males. This figure is higher than the one for the district (966) and for the State of Rajasthan as a whole (950). This is why the village has 403 male and 431 female voters.

Maps

There exists a map of the district of Chittorgarh indicating different Tehsils. It indicates the boundaries of other neighbouring districts, Bhilwara to the north, Rajsamand to the northwest, Udaipur to the west, and Banswara towards the south. On the eastern side, the district boundaries of Kapasan touch the State of Madhya Pradesh. Village Ranawaton-ki-Sadri lies on the western extreme in the middle of the district along the railway track connecting Udaipur and Chittorgarh. The map is helpful in locating some of the villages and towns with which the village gets connected for purposes of marriage and educational and economic opportunities.

Panchayat Samiti Records

The district map contains the names of important villages only, but for understanding its immediate connections with neighbouring villages, a detailed map of the Panchayat Samiti is more helpful. With main roads and pathways indicated and village boundaries clearly marked, it becomes a useful tool for locating both the villages connected in marriage relations as well as the boundaries over which inter-village administrative units operate.

The present village Panchayat, of which Ranawaton-ki-Sadri is a part, has its headquarters in the neighbouring village of Patoliya. The Panchayat area includes smaller settlements of Jawa, Anjan Kheda and Mundkatiya. The Panchayat membership of villages has undergone some changes since the first study; for example, Nilod and Pari now belong to another Panchayat. Constituencies for election to village Panchayat and representation in the Panchayat Samiti have been undergoing changes. The area over which Patwari has jurisdiction covers a number of villages; the headquarters of the revenue area are located in Kakarwa. It is from that centre that activities connected with the distribution of food grains to BPL families are conducted. The concept of BPL (Below the Poverty Line) was introduced much later to identify the families from various castes that deserve special provisions. The criteria for identification of the BPL families differ from state to state. Unlike the census enumeration, BPL families are those that apply for that status to the state authorities and that are admitted.[2]

As the village lies on the western border of the district, it has administrative connections with neighbouring villages and towns, particularly in Udaipur and Rajsamand districts, and their immediately neighbouring Tehsils of Mavli and Railmagra become significant. Maps of these two Tehsils are also significant. A number of specialised centres of worship mentioned by the villagers can be traced in the maps of the three Tehsils, which are obtained through different Panchayat Samiti offices.

Village Sketch Map

This map was prepared for this project jointly by the school teacher and Patwari in 2001. It is a sketch and is not according to scale.

The habitation map indicates the position of each house and numbering the same for indicating their type – *pakka* or *kachha*, main streets, places of worship, and pathways used for conducting the census and preparing the voters list. The map is useful in the study for locating the space occupied by groups of related families. Caste concentrations in different parts (mohallas) of the village can be seen in it. With the help of other information (courtesy the headmaster of the school), portions of newly constructed houses and localities were identified. The habitation pattern of the village constitutes Annexure 3.

Voters' List 2004

The voters list is an important document which provides relevant information about the voters: their age, sex and house number. For Ranawaton-ki-Sadri, 14 segments have been identified locating 834 named voters: 403 males and 431 females. The houses are serially numbered, making it easy to locate groups of units living in the compound. Names of the father or husband further help in finding connected families. The list is used primarily by political parties during elections. It is also helpful in planning developmental activities. We obtained the copy from the deputy Sarpanch of the village Panchayat.

Krishi Revenue Records – 2002

The land records of the village are maintained by the Patwari. These records carry information about all the plots of the land owned by the villagers. They also provide information about land cultivated by the villagers in other villages of the Tehsil. Information is available about 365 holdings for 208 owners whose names are recorded along with the father's name and caste. Information is separately available regarding (1) Scheduled Castes (SC), (2) Scheduled Tribes (ST), and (3) Other Backward Castes (OBC).

The document is useful for working on agrarian structure along families and castes. We obtained the document from the Tehsil office.

List of BPL Families

The consolidated list of families living Below Poverty Line (BPL) is prepared at the Panchayat Samiti level, an abstract for the village under study that includes serial numbers 3269–3368, indicating a total of 100 families. The list contains names of the heads of families, father's name and caste, and their social groups divided into five categories: (1) ST, (2) ST, (3) OBC, (4) Minorities and (5) General.

In the BPL card, information is available regarding ownership of land and classification of small/marginal farmers. The number of beneficiaries of the IRDP (Integrated Rural Development Programme) scheme is mentioned in the document. However, it must be hinted that the list of BPL families needs updating as it was prepared in 1997–1998; during the interregnum, status of many families might have changed. This exercise will help update the needed information and may serve as a corrective.

Pariwar Bank and Self-Help Groups

The formation of self-help groups (SHG) began in the village in the year 2001. These groups are small, 11–13 members, ensuring mutual understanding and converting it into a formal group and thus combining the advantages of primary and secondary groups in the new setting. In this case, the definition of rules of membership and process of working, their records become valuable source of information and are listed below:

(i) The *general rules of self-help groups* are laid down, and the list includes 10 points; these cover the rules for taking loans and define obligations of members. Provision is made for the election of president, treasurer and the secretary on an annual basis.

(ii) *The Pariwar Bank.* This is run by *Ma Bayan Mateshwari Samooh* and has 13 members who contribute ₹ 100 each per month. The bank was started on 15 April 2001.

Similar information is available for the following five other SHGs:

(a) Raj Laxmi Swayam Sahayata Samooh,

(b) Bhagya Laxmi SHG.

Both of these were opened on 10 December 2001.

Three groups were added in the year 2003:

(i) Vijay Laxmi SHG

(ii) Ohan Laxmi SHG

(iii) Vaibhav Laxmi SHG.

There is a procedure through which such groups can open an account in the bank. The Bank of Baroda serves this village, the branch of which is located in the neighbouring large village.

The Village Dairy

The dairy is run for collecting milk from the villagers and in turn making available better quality of cattle feed to the members. The collection of milk is controlled by the district body, and lists are maintained at the Tehsil and Panchayat Samiti levels. The Gram Panchayat of Patoliya has one collection centre in Ranawaton-ki-Sadri. The list of members, in effect, is a new census operation of the owners of the cattle and provides information on their names father/husband's name, castes, and their classification according to whether they belonged to SC, ST, OBC and General, their status as small and marginal farmers, and those who don't own any land. The animal census covers categories such as milch cattle, pregnant cattle and oxen.

The former Sarpanch of the village happens to head this committee; through his kind courtesy our team was able to obtain the list. The list contains names of *Pashu Palaks*, persons who rear the animals. The village has 128 *Pashu Palaks*. As many as 23 landless persons also applied for this designation, but they did not qualify because of lack of resources for maintaining cattle wealth. The document indicates how the census is undertaken, including groups classification of according to their castes, land resources and cattle wealth, and the selection criteria used for operating the scheme. The conduct of the scheme vests in an organisational setup independent of the Gram Panchayat activities and has links with the collection units at the Tehsil and district levels through whom payments are made directly and quite regularly through this special body.

School Records

Access to school records depends on a combination of factors. First, it depends on the care with which the headmaster keeps copies of records and his willingness to generate and consolidate information and, second, the level of trust between the investigators and the headmaster. Ready information was available on the enrolment of students according to sex. The information is available separately for SC, ST, and OBC students.

Upon request, the headmaster made available the list of students of class VIII over the previous three years along with a note on their current level of education or info on termination of education.

Information on significant stages of development of school and organization of the special events like interschool competitions, help received from various agencies like *Lok Jumbish*, Panchayat Samiti and grants given from MP (member of parliament) and MLA (member of legislative assembly) funds provided by the school.

The old building of the primary school is now used for *Anganwari*, where a space has been provided for children admitted for pre-primary schooling. The children and their mothers are provided free meals. Monthly meetings for SHGs are also held in the Anganwari campus.

Other State Agencies' Records

There is a *primary health sub-centre* in the village. Data on beneficiaries, type of assistance provided and allocation of resources by the state can be obtained through this centre.

There is also an Ayurvedic dispensary from where health-related basic information can be obtained.

Water, electricity and telephone bills are collected on allotted days, failing which the villagers have to go to the respective office centres to make the payments.

Researchers were able to obtain copies of the judgment from the District Magistrate Court. In our case, we obtained a copy of the judgment of a civil case (No. 65/99, CM 38). The case dealt with a Jat daughter from the village seeking divorce from her husband, invoking Section 13 of the Hindu Marriage Act. The judgment covers legal as well as customary aspects of the case culminating in the acceptance of the suit. The final outcome was the remarriage of the girl according to customary practices in which the girl's brother-in-law took the initiative. The document contained valuable information on custom and law in the rural setting. The copy of the judgment was obtained through the courtesy of the advocate from the village.

The increasing availability of records adds to the authenticity of the data, clarifies the role of agencies that maintain them and calls for special efforts on the part of investigators to collect the same. The sources of information can be treated to generate special tables and arriving at interpretations of various types, depending on the aspects that social researchers consider worthwhile beyond the purpose for which the data were collected or recorded by different agencies.

Attention may now be given to the type of data collected by the investigators during the process of the study in the following section.

Field Techniques

1. *Genealogical chart.* The study in historical depth beginning with the foundation of the village through the arrival of Zorawar Singh and his two sons provides the starting point for the genealogical chart for the *Rajput* families and covers eight descending generations who now constitute 40 family units in the village (Annexure 4). The two sons of the founder have given rise to the two lineages or sub-lineages. The rule of primogeniture has been followed for determining the lineage of the chief locally called the Thakur Sahib, who continues to live in the fortress-like structure called the Rawla. The younger son was the first to move out of the building; he built his house in the cattle yard (*Nohra*). Further differentiation with the multiplication of younger sons and their families resulted in the formation of new compounds for living. Every member today has some sort of urban contacts and details regarding them can be traced through the schedule administered on a family basis. However, the links among the families can be traced through the genealogical chart which now serves as a ready reckoner even for the members of the caste in the village. The genealogical chart prepared by our team is used for understanding the nature of traditional links, identity formation, and competitive political behaviour.
2. *Household schedule.* A three-page schedule was developed to record details about each member of family, including age, occupation, place of work and marital connections. The entry regarding grandfather's name further helped to link the connected

families and read along with the genealogical chart to understand the depth of links. The data covered size of landholdings, agricultural instruments, cattle wealth and new household goods. These depict the urban impact on the lifestyles of the inhabitants.

3. *Observations in the village of origin.* Zorawar Singh had to leave the main village of Sanwad after having dispute with the other brother regarding the inheritance of the Jagir. The main palace-like structure in Sanwad, the village of origin, has the outer and the inner gates that are huge enough for elephants to enter the court yard. The palatial building had a temple for the presiding deity of the lineage – *Bayan Mata*.

   In the administrative setting of the princely order the village of Sanwad occupied the rank of the second order called *Battisa* or 32, and the first order consisted of 16 villages. The present incumbent was interviewed at length to trace and document the history of the lineage. Members of the lineally related families currently living in Ranawaton-ki-Sadri were aware of the spread of the lineages and the marriage connections as well as personal characteristics of members of the Sanwad family.

4. *Videography.* The team also did videography for a better comprehension of the layout of the palace and its surroundings, including the railway station of Fateh Nagar, and the habitat of the village under-study. The filming of the *Rawala* as well as three other important compounds helped us understand the manner in which the space was redistributed for use by the Rajput families upon their separation. A few *Rajput* families were covered by the video as also the

important streets. Important places of worship in the village were filmed. Some of the festivities were also covered in the process. A peculiar event of combined worship of all the deities of the village at *Lal Mata* was also filmed. In another round, shots of the village school were taken, and shots of the bird's eye view of the village and performances of the *Gavri* and *Jaljhulni Ekadashi* were also taken. These events form a special feature of the video film and helped greatly in the conduct of the case study.

5. *Case studies.* A combination of observation and interviews has been used to study few select rituals that occurred during the period of inquiry. The video film helped in describing the *Kheda Devat* – village deities – and also the role of various attendants and worshippers. Over a period of time the deities get known for their charismatic effect, which has to be demonstrated periodically to demonstrate steadfast devotion. Here one sees a process of the rise and decline of the respect for deities among the followers. The new centres of supernatural power were also located by the research team. At the time of elections, various contending candidates went to these religious abodes to seek the blessings of the reigning deity. Within the village a colourful Shiva temple has recently been built with the help of the school headmaster and the contractor engaged by the Indian railways to convert meter gauge train track into broad gauge. Villagers have been making contributions to their specific caste deities. These participatory observations have helped in understanding the process of enhanced reutilisation, to which reference was first made in *A Rajasthan Village* (1967).

Case studies of rituals conducted by the team cover rituals performed by the people on the second day of Dewali. This day is observed as a day of worship of the cattle-wealth. It combines collective activities organised at four centres in the village depicting its community character in terms of participating actors. The *Jaljhulni Ekadashi* and connected tribal festival involving the dance-drama (*Gavri*) have also been observed to understand the pattern of inter-caste interaction.

Observation of the life cycle rituals – *rites de passage* – provided a good deal of material to supplement the interviews. In fact, the researcher was helped in preparing probing questions to gather more comprehensive details about rituals. The team was able to observe during the course of field work a marriage ceremony and also a case of death which provided an opportunity to witness eschatological rituals among the Rajput caste. During the field work a remarriage that took place in the Jat community was also observed.

6. *Life histories.* Every community has persons who play an important part in village activities. They contribute to the observance of the norms as well as to the modernization of village activities in various spheres. They ensure continuity of the village's culture on one side and serve as agents of change on the other. The research team prepared three such life histories; these relate to: (a) a Sarpanch who had a tenure of three terms, (b) a resident lawyer who commutes to work at the Tehsil headquarters and (c) the headmaster of the government middle school. Each of these village

leaders has contributed a good deal in the modernization of the village community.

Conducting field study requires a combination of various tools of inquiry. The existence of multiple sources enables one to cross-check information and helps develop a social profile of the rural life.

Notes

1. Various Jagirs in Mewar and other princely states in Rajasthan maintain such records of their lineages. Agencies such as the ICSSR and ICHR are obtaining copies of these records in their documentation centres.
2. Researchers have hinted at the weakness of the tool, and at the deficiencies in identifying the "real" BPL families. Many non-deserving BPL families are enjoying this privilege and several deserving cases are left out.

2

The Village

The manner in which the lineage of Ranawats got established in the village and influenced the development of the hamlet has been described in detail in my first book on this village, which was published in 1967. In this monograph, the focus shifted from the manner in which groups of families linked to the Ranawat lineage have further diversified within the village and the manner in which the village property has been redistributed with the growth of kin group to the onset of modernisation processes.

Today, the Ranawats live in 11 different compounds in the village. Similarly, the caste of Gadri, which Atal has named Gairy, a caste of herdsmen, lives in seven such compounds. The Jat, another agricultural caste whose males are also called Patel, live in three distinct compounds. The Bhil – a tribal caste settled in the village – have nine lineages, of which the *Mothi* is the predominant section. Very few people can recite the growth of families in each lineage beyond three to four generations of ancestors.

As was mentioned earlier, Ranawats got separated from the Shaktavat clan because of differences between the Ranawat King Maharana Pratap and his younger brother, Shakti Singh. The latter claimed the inheritance which Maharana Udai Singh denied. In fact, one other Maharani wanted her son to succeed, but the Rajput nobles favoured Pratap Singh and took him with them to Gogunda for his coronation. It is believed that later the two brothers patched up their differences but branched off in two separate clans. The descendants of Maharana continued to be called Ranawat, and the descendants of Shakti Singh formed the new lineage called Shaktavat.

All the Ranawats belong to the main exogamous group (an equivalent of Gotra or clan) called *Shishodiya* or *Guhilot* (also called *Gehlot* – descendant of the King Guhil who is said to have founded the kingdom of Mewar, with Chittorgarh as its capital). Knowables of the history of Mewar possess greater details of the kinship divisions within the royal family of Mewar.

The re-study of the village Ranawaton-ki-Sadri in 2003–2004 on which the present report is based has focused on the *extension of space*. There has been a good deal of construction activity; increasing number of family units has spread out and constructed new houses and improved cattle yards (called *Nohras).* The Nohras serve both as the added living space and the storehouse for keeping agricultural implements and crops brought from the fields. The extended area provides space for meeting visitors and for lodging guests. The *Nohra* is also used for social gatherings of men and for negotiating business deals. Family feasts are also held there. Construction and improvements of the facilities within the residential compounds and the *Nohra* are continuing features of life in the village. The renovated parts of the house and the

Nohras serve as indicators of modernisation. They also signify the changing status of their dwellers.

The village has not suffered from the 'talent-drain'. Not many people have moved from the village to urban areas. However, those who have taken up jobs or started their own businesses in urban areas constitute definitely a distinct class of migrants. Barring a few families, most people who went out of the village for earning a living have returned to the village to lead the life of retirement. Their children, however, live elsewhere for work.

The outside exposure and earnings from the non-agricultural sources have helped revitalise the rural base. Since the village is very close to the urban metropolis of Udaipur and the growing township of Chittorgarh, the villagers working there do not feel the need to permanently shift their inherited location. Improved roads and easy availability of affordable means of transport served to retain the village population. Besides, many features of the city are also arriving in the village. These serve as disincentives to settle elsewhere. That is why the number of families who have migrated from this village has remained minimal. Urban amenities are reaching the village and, as a consequence, modernising the little community like the one under study. The urban way of life has begun influencing the people in villages.

The Space and the People

Over the years, the village has grown in size. Both space and social groups associated with each other get noted in a variety of ways. The village has 834 voters of whom 403 are males and 431 females; these constitute the adult population of the village.[1] The population of the village is distributed over 13 'segments' as indicated in the sketch map (Annexure 2).

The neighbourhoods or mohallas were named after the predominant caste. However, five sections of the village are named after the characteristics of soil or with reference to a significant landmark.

There seems to be an even distribution of males and females in the various parts of the village. Only in two of the segments the number of male voters exceeds that of females. Of these two, one locality is recently established in the southern part of the village. Other segments have equal number of male and female voters. Three segments are marked on consideration of the vicinity of the houses and are identified along caste names; in eight other cases, the neighbourhood is named after the preponderant group. Names of other mohallas consist of references like those connected with the colour of the stone: white (*Dhaula*) or black (*Kala*) or just the rocky street (*Khakhariya*). *Khala Chaperda* is a place where *Khala* or common thrashing ground was located. The locality near the temple is called '*Mandir ke Pass*', that is, near the temple. The classification of segments suggests identification of social groups in respective areas predominantly, though not exclusively. The distribution of sectors is shown on a sketch map of the village.

Calculations were done independently by identifying voters' castes, and comparing their concentration in different sectors indicated that in each living area (Mohalla) two out of eleven voters belong to other castes. This helped us infer that the population in the sectors demarcated for voting purposes was heterogeneous in terms of caste composition.

The Land and the People

The total land of the village as per Patwari records is 581.55 hectares, of which 539.82 hectares is distributed among 274 landholdings. The major portion of these holdings is in the name of residents in 269 family units covering 82 per cent of the area for which an annual rent of ₹ 5892.20 is charged. Together with the income from three holdings spread over 8.54 hectares, the total revenue from the village thus comes to ₹ 5898.32. A total of 41.73 (35.14%) hectares of land is not available for cultivation, the major portion of which (42.86%) is covered by roads and pathways and 22 per cent by habitation. The remaining area consists of fallow land, streams, the burning Ghat (cremation ground), and wasteland.

During the *Kharif* season of 2003–2004 crops were grown over 242.32 hectares. The major crop is (maize/corn) was sown in 62.3 per cent of the land. Maize is staple food for people in the region. Among pulses sown in 22.02 hectares, *Urad* covers the major portion, 83.2 per cent, and the remaining land (one-fourth of the land) is used for sowing *Moong*. Oil seeds are sown in twice the area used for the pulses. Production of groundnut has gained currency in recent years. The closer proximity to Fateh Nagar as a *Mandi* (wholesale market) dealing in oil has been a key factor in the promotion of groundnut crop in the region.

For example, over a period of five years ending 1999–2000, production of groundnut in the district of Chittorgarh increased three-fold, which achieved a six-fold increase later (District Statistical Outline, 2000–2001, p. 36). Whereas the general production of the *Til* (sesame) for the district was only 1105 metric tons for the year 1999, it was 19,756 tons for groundnuts, that is, 18 times that of sesame. For the Tehsil of Kapasan, the difference was eleven times. While the general direction appears to be favouring groundnut over *Til*, the spread of the former in the village is slower than in the surrounding villages of the region.

The differential distribution of land ownership, according to various caste groups, would provide an idea of the manner in which the most important asset in agricultural community contributes to the economy of these groups.

Let us look into the distribution of the village population first.

The census of the village conducted by our team in the first round covered twelve castes among which the number of families and the number of persons present a slightly different picture. In the first three castes having more than 20 families in the village, the *Gadri* ranked top followed by the *Bhil* and the *Rajput*. On the other hand, as one comes to the number of persons, the situation is reversed: the *Rajput* are on top and the *Gadri* are in the third position; the *Bhil* ranked second in both cases. The ranking remains the same with regard to average size of the family; the *Rajput* accounting for 7.95 per cent, *Bhil* 4.55 per cent and Gadri 4.09 per cent.

The difference is not related to fertility but probably to longevity and composition of the family.

The distribution of the twelve castes according to family and persons is shown in Table 2.1.

Table 2.1

Number of families and persons according to castes in the village in 2003

No.	Caste	Number of families	Percentage in the total	Number of persons	Percentage in the total
1.	Gadri	55	26.70	225	21.31
2.	Bhil	53	25.73	241	22.82
3.	Rajput	40	19.42	318	30.11
4.	Jat (Patel)	18	8.74	61	5.78
5.	Jatia	11	5.34	55	5.21
6.	Khatik	09	4.36	69	6.53
7.	Jaiswal	06	2.91	20	1.89
8.	Bairagi	04	1.94	16	1.52
9.	Daroga	03	1.46	10	0.94
10.	Kumhar	03	1.46	16	1.52
11.	Kharol	02	0.97	13	1.23
12.	Teli	02	0.97	12	1.13
	Total	206	100.00	1056	100.00

Data gathered by the research team in 2003.

The characteristic features of the first twelve castes are described in detail in Chapters 3 and 4.

The second round of census covered the remaining caste groups with five families of the *Suthar* and one of the *Nai*. Among the new arrivals in the recent period are two *Keer* families associated with growing vegetables and fruit-creepers in the river bed. They came on their own and purchased the land belonging to the *Mahajan* who had left the village for better prospects in Gujarat. One *Meghwal* family also came to the village and continued its traditional work of procuring the hides. The family lives in a rented house near the flourmill towards the southern end. A *Rajput* belonging to the Shaktawat clan came from Bhindar to look after the sale of liquor on behalf of a contractor. His shop is a kilometre south of *Dhaula Danta* locality. He also resides there. The *Dholi* for the village is the son of the migrant from the nearby Tehsil town of Kapasan. He was married to a family in *Anjan Kheda* hamlet and stayed there as the original family was left without an heir. This serving group works as a village drummer; members of this group are hired for all important occasions in the village for all the castes other than the *Rajput*. For the latter caste, a Dholi comes from Sanwad.

The lone *Lohar* (Ironsmith) family is represented by a widow.

There are two scavengers (until recently also called *Harijan*) families in the village. Two boys of this caste have gone to Udaipur to work as peons in a hostel. One middle-aged person, his wife and children perform sweeping tasks for the *Rajput* families, besides sweeping the village street. In return for the domestic services, the family is given cooked food daily, besides a monthly payment from the Rajput households. The daughter of this family is currently studying in 10th class in the nearby village of Patoliya where her brother also studies in 5th class – a change worthy of note. Their house has electricity; the family also maintains a kitchen garden. The rooms in the house are maintained neatly, and the family owns a transistor radio. TV has not yet arrived in the village.

Incidentally, the family does not carry the night soil, as people go out to answer their nature's call in the jungle or the fields.

Families of the three caste groups have left the village to live elsewhere. But the village has also received services in the traditional sector from one family which migrated from the nearby village of Sanwad and allowed three other families from another village to settle here. These families offer their services to nearby villages as well.

Caste-wise land distribution suggests that Rajput families own most of the land, followed by the *Gadri* and the Jat. The latter two castes arrived and settled at the asking of the village chief in the early period of establishing the village in order to augment the productivity of soil and more revenue from the crop. Population-wise, the *Bhil* who were ranked second in population size, have slipped to fourth position. Jats have most of the irrigated land followed by the *Rajput* and the *Gadri*. The position of other castes are illustrated clearly in Table 2.2.

With virtually no rainfall over the first three years of the twenty-first century, the village Thakur's family used the tank-beds for growing crops. In 2004, a torrential rain flooded the village tanks and other water resources, and it also destroyed the corn (maize) crop. However, heavy rain prepared the fields for the next crop in the ensuing year.

The villagers took steps to store water in the third tank. It became a happy sight for all. The villagers rejoiced the bounty and celebrated festivals, particularly the *Jal Jhulni Ekadashi*, with a big fanfare. For day-to-day needs, the tank serves as a source of water facilitating bath, washing clothes and even enabling people to ease themselves in the neighbouring shrubs – people still prefer to go in the open for discharge of night soil and use water resources for ablution.

Table 2.2

Caste-wise distribution of land owned and irrigated

	Caste	*Total family*	*Land owned (bigha)*	*Average*	*Land irrigated (bigha)*	*Average pertaining (bigha)*
1.	Rajput	40	890	22.25	196	4.90
2.	Bairagi	04	12	03.00	00	0.00
3.	Gadri	55	440	08.00	255	4.63
4.	Khatik	09	34	03.77	31	3.44
5.	Daroga		36	01.00	02	0.66
6.	Kharol	02	08	04.00	08	4.00
7.	Teli	02	11	05.50	00	0.00
8.	Kumhar	03	16	05.33	11	3.66
9.	Deshwal	06	33	05.50	33	5.50
10.	Patel	18	321	17.83	144	8.00
11.	Jatia	11	43	03.90	27	2.45
12.	Bhil	53	121	02.28	96.5	1.82

Data collected by the research team as part of the household survey.

The overall man-land balance in the village puts the Rajput in a dominant position in the community. They are the largest in size and upper-most in social ranking. It is worthy of note that the village has no *Brahmin* family.

To the features of dominance, what needs be added is that the access to educational and economic opportunities in the urbanising sector now plays a significant part in village social structure. The Rajputs, thus, provide a pool for the leadership as well as challenges for power. It is important to note that all of the castes have begun responding to urban challenges, and the young among them are in search of better opportunities on their own in the modern urban sector. The results, however, vary in different caste groups and partly get reflected in the house types as shown in the habitation sketch diagram. The phenomenon of rural-urban interactions has been the core concern of analysis in the subsequent chapters.

It may, however, be said at this stage that caste configurations present a ready reference for understanding the trends in the growing secular sector of life and their own identity gets strengthened through the rituals they observe.

Note

1. In 1955, when the village was first studied, its population was 640 (349 males, and 291 females). Now the voters alone are 834 in number. One can estimate that the population of the village now must be more than one thousand.

3

Social Profiles I

The Ranawats

The earlier study of this village, published in 1968, was based on intensive fieldwork. It depicts the profile of the village of the late 1950s. The book based on that fieldwork depicted the history of settlement in the manner in which it went on adding more families from different caste groups over time, contributing heterogeneity to the village. The present work carries the time dimension further back, tracing every connecting link to the founders of the lineage and looks into the developments that had occurred over the past five decades with particular emphasis on the lineage, growth of households and reshaping of 'compounds'.[1]

As was said earlier, the name of the village is associated with the *Ranawat* family of the *Rajput* caste who were the first to settle here. The name suggests the origin of the lineage from the royal family of Mewar. The ruler of this state was the only one who was addressed as 'Rana' or 'Maharana' because of his refusal to submit to the dictates of Mughal rulers. The legend has it that the young prince named Udai Singh was born in Chittorgarh and that his mother's brother tried to assassinate him. Knowing about this conspiracy, the lactating nurse named *Panna Dhai* took the prince and her own son in a bamboo basket to escape from the palace. She was looking after the infant Udai Singh as well as her own son. Both of them were kept in improvised baskets and she tried to take them out to a safer haven. But she was caught while escaping. When the attackers asked her to identify the prince she pointed her finger at her own son who was, without further verification killed on the spot, and the nurse was then allowed to escape with her son. This way the nurse made great sacrifice of her own child and saved the heir to the throne of Mewar, who was secretly taken to another fort of Kumbhalgarh, more than 100 kilometres to the northwest of Chittorgarh.

Udai Singh, it may be recalled, was one of the four sons of the legendary Maharana Sanga. At the battlefield of 'Khanwah' Sanga was defeated by Babar (1527). Maharana Sanga died soon. He was succeeded by two sons in arow, each occupying the throne successively for short durations. The fourth son, Udai Singh, who was saved by Panna Dhai, took the reins of Mewar and ruled the kingdom for a longer duration of 32 years (1540–1572). His son Pratap Singh opted for a safer capital city and founded the new capital Udaipur. Maharana Udai Singh had 23 queens and got two sons from one of them, and one each from the rest, as the villagers say. The court historian Shyamal Das authenticates 18 queens of whom 24 princes were born (1889, p. 87; Annexure 3). One of the princes later became the most famous king of Mewar – Maharana Pratap Singh. Viram Dev was the third prince branching off from the brother, the crown prince. His lineage was called Ranawat. The descendants of the second prince Shakti Singh call themselves Shaktawat. All of them are subsets of Shishodia clan. The nomenclature of lineage from the brothers of the crown prince helps in identification of the each parting point from the group and serves as a ready reckoner for practising clan exogamy: thus different sections of Shishodia will not marry in any other Shishodia lineages. The descendants of Viram Dev call themselves Viramdevot and continue to retain the wider appellation Ranawat.

Viram Dev had three sons, who occupied seven villages. On migration from Chittorgarh, the third son lsardas moved to a neighbouring village Ghosunda, which is now the first railway station connecting Chittorgarh to Udaipur. Over a period of time, the descendants of Viram Dev acquired the Jagir of Sanwad, 55 kilometres to the west of Chittorgarh. His younger brothers moved to seven different villages of the erstwhile Jagir. This lineage is growing and practices exogamy. While separated as economic units, these families are a dominant political group. Knowledge about the strength and weakness of the members of the brotherhood (*Bhai-Bandh*) also get shared and relations of intimacy may be defined by the ego of the concerned. The most well-known family in the second quarter of the twentieth century came from the village Kakarwa. One of the descendants of this family became a Judicial Officer and Chief Justice of the Princely State of Mewar. On the merger of the state with the wider Rajasthan in the late 1940s, he became the first Chief Justice of Rajasthan. His son, though less educated, joined politics but turned out to be a failure. Another member of Kakarwa family became an IAS officer. He was instrumental in improving water supply in the two villages with the introduction of modern plants.

From the village Kuncholi has emerged a historian of recognised merit, named Manohar Singh Ranawat. He is currently the director of a well-established Natnagar Sansthan, founded by the prince of Sitamau in the neighbouring state of Madhya Pradesh. Scholars working on the history of Malwa use that centre as an important source of references. In this regard, mention may be made of the works of Adrian C. Mayer (London School of African and Oriental Studies) and of K.S. Mathur (Department of Anthropology, University of Lucknow) who frequented this centre for consulting historical records.

Zoravar Singh, in the seventh descending generation from Viram Dev, had branched off from Sanwad to Sadri – village under study – and obtained control of the village through a conquest of the Bhat head who offered resistance. He occupied the well-built *pucca* house as it had enough space for the invading family. The brother of Zoravar Singh lived separately and was addressed by the villagers as *Maharaj* out of sheer respect. Zoravar Singh had two sons P.S. and S.M.; the descendants of the first one got the village in succession and were addressed by the villagers as *Thakur*. According to the rule of primogeniture, the eldest son succeeds the headship of the village. In the absence of an heir-apparent, either the brother of the dead, or his son, ascends the throne through adoption.

During the first study of the village (1956), J.S. was the Thakur[2]; the present-day (2004) Thakur belongs to the fourth descending generation. Thus, the ruling clan continues to hold power.[3]

The founding chief (J.S.) had a son named S.M. The latter had five sons. The families descended from the common ancestor residing in front of the small fortress called the *Rawala*, which is occupied by the present head of the lineage. A section of that lineage built their own bungalow near the fields in *Anjankheda*; the breakaway group came to be known as '*bangla wala*'. From there a breakaway group migrated to Namboda village in the same district. Another section – the descendants of the branched-off families – resides in the north-eastern part and is referred to by the villagers as '*Nohra wala*'. The old cattle yard (*Nohra*) was renovated when this breakaway group moved there to reside. One of the members of this breakaway group joined the police service as a sub-inspector. Upon his retirement, he returned to the village and engaged in agriculture with the installation of improved agricultural tools. People called him *Thanedar Saheb* (Police Inspector). His son got engaged himself in contractual jobs besides being a progressive farmer.

The main lineage of the founder Zoravar Singh was perpetuated through P.S., and the next in line, D.S., had an illustrious successor in Ram Singh who built columns in four corners and a surrounding wall on all sides of the residential compound to give it the shape of a fortress – *Rawla*. The similarity of the pattern of this *Rawla* with the one in the villages of origin in Sanwad is quite striking. Outside the dwelling unit is a space marked for the stable of the horses on the right side, and on the left kept for keeping fodder. The house has a decorated main palatial entrance. Jutting out of the main building is a covered and raised platform for the guests. The space is also used for playing cards, gossips and other recreational activities for the males. Towards the right is a temple for the family goddess Bayan Mata. In between is the passage where the Thakur spent his day relaxing and keeping a general watch on movements. The growth of the ruling family required constant redefinition of the living area.

The children of the ruling household had nominal education. In the third generation of the migrating Thakur family, there was B.S. who studied better[3] and was able to become the headmaster of the middle school. Another member, T.S., served as *Faujdar*, whose task was to serve as a linkman between the village Thakur and villagers. Later, he was co-opted as a caretaker of the village Panchayat. The third son, K.S., also assisted in keeping law and order in the village. The three sons lived in a compact block on the western side of the *Rawla*, which was popularly referred to as *Chhota Rawla*, while Ram Singh, the eldest son of J.S., continued to live in the *Rawla*, and the other brothers – P.S., V.S. and G.S. – established their own residences in the eastern side of the *Rawla*. They constitute the second order in the *Rajput* lineage in the village. The five sons of J.S. moved out of the *Rawla* to the new site called 'Navi Jagah' (new place), towards the North-West of the *Rawla*. A common entrance gate with separate residences inside for each family redefined the new compound. It was on the left side of the gate on a raised platform that the researcher used to stay during the course of the first inquiry. Four decades later, the same space was used by the new team of researchers.

Further growth in the family units required construction of new rooms both within the compound and at other landed property. Two of the families extended their residence to 'Khala Chaparda' – the place where 'Khala', grains used to be thrashed. That collective activity also got diversified to individual plots of land and is now conducted speedily through thrashers. The space thus vacated has been used for extension of the residential area. To this general space, two families from the eastern side of the *Rawla* have also moved. All the new residences look modern.

This sector of the village has the middle school further west; and in between the new houses and the old site an Ayurvedic dispensary and a sub centre of Primary Health Services have been located. A few other houses from the '*Chhota Rawla*' also occupy this area. The residences and buildings are separately identifiable. These may be called neighbourhoods rather than compounds, as members have a tendency to treat themselves as family units. The connections with the parental houses in the old compound are, however, maintained.

The two sub-lineages living on the eastern side of the *Rawla* and the 'Navi Jagah' and beyond provide the most educated section of the *Rajputs* of the village. They represent the characteristic growth of the younger brothers of the village chief in the system of primogeniture. The residents of the eastern part of the 'Rawla' initiated the move with P.S. becoming a forest ranger, succeeded by his son, who was also in a similar capacity. Both were continued to be addressed as 'Ranger Sahib' even after their retirement. He has three sons; one is running a tourist trade in Udaipur and the other lives in Jodhpur. The eldest of the three is an advocate who resides in the village and commutes to work at the headquarters of the Panchayat Samiti and the Tehsil. He has played the key role of friend, philosopher and guide for developmental works in the village and surrounding units. He is the president of the district cell for advocates of the BJP, the ruling party in the state. He successfully sought election to the membership of the Panchayat Samiti through the neighbouring constituency of Pari and adjoining villages in the year 2000. He is *Pradhan* of the Samiti. His active role in the development of the village consists in getting cement concrete streets within the village, upgrading of a primary school into a middle school and installation of two drinking-water tanks. He provides the link with the administration and the Panchayat Samiti. As a practising advocate, he is influential at the Tehsil level and was particularly helpful to the investigating team for making copies of various official records available. He thinks positively about development of the village and is active in organising internal and external resources through his links. His dream project is to get a centralised water supply tank involving expenditure in six figures.

V.S., the second brother of Thakur J.S., had joined as the administration officer after graduating in agricultural sciences from Jobner. His son became the headmaster of the government school in the initial stages of its growth and helped it to grow into a higher secondary school at a new site in the neighbouring town of Fateh Nagar. The school has spacious playgrounds and buildings. Upon retirement, he returned to his parental village.

The next generation diversified. One of his sons became a lawyer, and his wife joined the teaching profession. Another son joined the tourist trade in Udaipur, and the third son became a physical instructor in the government school. The fourth brother was the first to have moved to the outer edge of this *Rawla* to live separately.

His descendants constitute another line in assisting Jagir administration. The first son, Zoravar Singh, did not continue his studies but played a role in administering the

Jagir. Upon his death, his widow – Anand Kunwar – was chosen as the Sarpanch of the village in 1995. It may be mentioned here that this seat is reserved for women. One of her sons teaches in a government school, another joined the railways and his son became a truck driver. The descendants in this lineage deal in oil business. The third son of the village chief – now 73 years of age – had studied in Udaipur up to eighth standard and became a Patwari. However, after serving for two years he re-joined the school to clear the tenth standard. He chose the career of a sportsperson, playing of football at the state level. Later, the railways picked him up and appointed him as a loco driver. He narrated to our research team several details of the village history during his life time.

His son, Thakur Amar Singh, was also a good player. He was similarly picked up by the railways services and retired as a driver. The next in line, T.S., also studied commerce at B.N. College, Udaipur, then well-known as a centre for promoting games and sports. Along with another fellow villager – son of the headmaster – went for training in physical education at Amravati in Maharashtra. Upon completion of their training both became physical instructors in schools. This shifting of occupational work in the Thakur's lineage is indicative of the multiple roles that incumbents have simultaneously begun to play. While continuing to discharge responsibilities at home, they have engaged in jobs in the modern sector. This pattern has its parallel in the village that was studied by Daniel Lerner and recorded in his famous book *The Passing of Traditional Society* (1964). Like the situation in Lerner's village, the descendants of the Thakur's family were also the first to enter into government jobs leaving the village and getting exposure to modern education. The children of the families of the old order become pace setters in a changing milieu.

As families within a 'compound' grow in number and size, the compounds were modified to have new gates to reach out into the village. Addition of *apertures* – to use Atal's coinage[4] – to the walls of the village compound is an indicator of 'opening out' and the expansion of lineage lodged in the old compound. Thus, M.S. opened new entrances to the north of the *Rawala*, descendants of P.S and V.S. opened out towards the east and the 'Nohra Wala' unit created an aperture towards the south facing the *Rawala*. Similar extensions occurred in the new site named 'Navi Jagah' towards the south and the west; the 'Chhota Rawala' got an opening on the western side. The surrounding walls of the compound no longer necessitate a common entry–exit point although the old main gate structure still exists and used for receiving the guests and for playing indoor games by family elders. On ceremonial occasions like reception or departure of the *Barat* (marriage party) the large gates are decorated as the main entry point to the compound.

The housing patterns of important castes are given at Annexure 5.

In the year 2004, there were 40 families of the Ranawats in the village. All these families can be dotted on a genealogical chart tracing backwards to Zoravar Singh, the founder of the lineage and the first Thakur of the village. A single genealogical chart running up to 3.20 metres was prepared by the research team in which all the male members of these families – covering five generations – were properly located. The rule of primogeniture employed for succession to the chief's position in the village had ensured continuity of the chiefdom being maintained wholly on the basis of the Jagir. In the sixth generation the person who would become the chief had also studied up to class 10 and has been selected for a job in the railways. It may be mentioned in the passing that he was the second son of the chief, but because of the death of his elder brother he became the lawful successor of the Jagir and was addressed as Thakur.

It may be said that the seventh generation, the current one, represents the more decisive step in acquiring mobility and diversification through the pursuit of education up to graduation level along with training in physical education and getting a state job in the school in the neighbourhood. The care of former Jagir lands and acquisition of new skills in a combined manner bring forth the new trend in a traditional village polity. The younger sons seek their opportunities in the wider world mainly through education and going for dignified occupations, like teaching and administration. The members of this lineage constitute the upper stratum on the scale of development in terms of power, prestige and wealth. A little bit of diversification along managerial positions in tourism and entry into the legal profession has brought in elements of the white-collar tradition in the lifestyles of the people of the so-called ruling household. This group of families were earlier associated with assisting Jagir administration in small ways, and their public contacts made them take up leadership tasks at the local level with an indifferent orientation of the illiterate village dwellers. Gradually, however, when it became clearer that in the new political setup candidature for election for the parliament or the state assembly was beyond their capacities, later even the Zila Parishad position was rather deemed distant, and the local elite started taking active interest in affairs connected with multi-village Panchayat and constituency for the membership of the Panchayat Samiti.

In the recent past, the main lineage became active in the development of the village, but a sort of competitive politics entered the scene with two sections of the lineage aligning themselves with two leading political parties at the state and the national level. In this process, mobilisation of support from other castes and villages has acquired a new dynamism of its own. It would be simplistic to state today that the Ranawats constitutes the dominant group in the village. It has also to be underscored that the group provides the pool for leadership to diverse forces and that manipulability skills are in operation requiring contacts with other castes, villages and parties.

Notes

1. In his study of Pul Eliya (1961) Leach attempted such an exercise.
2. A clarification of the term *Thakur* is necessary, as in Rajasthan it relates to the position of the chief of the village and there can be only one in the village, unlike the usage of the term in UP and Bihar where it is an appellation for people of the Rajput caste. As a prefix to the name, however, the term is used among the Rajput only for the member of the first generation, Kunwar for the second, and Bhanwer for the third, and the passing away of a generation lifts the designation one up. The 'Bhanwar' becoming a 'Kunwar', and the 'Kunwar' becomes the 'Thakur'.
3. The two lineages became competitive in the political arena by joining two opposing parties – the Congress Party and Bhartiya Janta Party (BJP).

4. See, Yogesh Atal, *Entering the Global Village: Essays on the Sociology of Communication*, particularly the Chapter 8 titled, 'Insulators and Apertures: Dynamics of Nation Building' (Rawat Publications, Jaipur, 2008). This essay was delivered as the Fourth Mahatma Gandhi Memorial Lecture at the University of London in May 1972.

4

Social Profiles II

Other Castes in the Village

Villagers now maintain active contacts with urban areas in two ways. They go to towns for higher studies or for acquiring new skills. They also migrate to urban areas for getting jobs in the industrial/corporate sector of the economy. Over the past half a century, townships have been growing in the region, and their effects are visible in the neighbouring villages. Most of the towns are just overgrown villages; these have brought in several traits to transform village lifestyle into urban lifestyle. Electrification, road connectivity, availability of modern means of transport, modern means of communication – beginning with the arrival of battery-operated transistor sets, and now the mobile phones – and increasing literacy, particularly among the younger age groups, have contributed to this transformation. Changes in the rural-urban continuum, and migration to urban centres have, thus, affected the village culture and social structures. Improvements in transportation and communication have made rural-urban contacts more varied and frequent.

In the village under study, besides the Rajput families people of two other castes have set up their small establishments in nearby urban areas. Persons belonging to the caste of Sadhu, for example, left the village and settled first in a nearby small town and later on moved further to a bigger city. Some members of this migrant family ultimately left for the Gulf Countries for better job prospects.

Similarly, persons belonging to the Khatik caste – traditionally engaged in butchery, similar to Muslim Qureshi – moved out of the village giving up their traditional vocation and undertaking new chores for earning a living. They are a living example of the process of *Sanskritisation* (a concept coined by Srinivas) in the sense that they gave up their traditional occupation, adopted vegetarianism and began observing Hindu rituals and practices. This facilitated their upward climbing. Their exposure to Western and modern way of life and adoption of other means of earning a livelihood helped erase the stereotype associated with their caste. Similarly, the Jat, who are primarily agriculturists, have begun sending their children for higher studies in nearby urban areas. Rather than returning to the village and getting engaged in the traditional vocation of agriculture, they are now engaged in urban jobs such as running the tempos – mechanised vehicles – in the neighbouring town. Of course, some have taken up managerial roles in agriculture rather than doing agriculture themselves or grazing their sheep and cattle.

It must, however, be emphasised that the urban out-migration has not resulted in the severance of ties with the village of origin. Those who work abroad continue to maintain their ties with their kith and kin who are still residing in the village. They also use food crops grown in their fields for personal consumption and only sell the remainder in the market. Some also grow cash crops, such as tobacco, groundnut and the like. The well-to-do families have acquired mechanised modes of transport – such as scooters and motorcycles – through which they commute between their village and the urban places of work.

The second aspect of urbanisation is visible in urban influences reaching the village in styles of consumption with improved houses, electric connections and appliances like the fans, TV and telephone. The number of *pakka* houses has grown up and a few sanitary comforts added. The presence of retired persons and their concerns for the growth of the third generation are a feature of the village life. A dozen of daily newspapers reach the village. Besides, several families listen to radio/transistor or watch TV – the new acquisitions for entertainment and news. It is important to mention that these media have partially done away with the need for literacy. The tribal families of the Bhils living in the village now take up work on daily wages in neighbouring towns. They generally use bicycles to commute between the village and the places of work in neighbouring villages. Effects of urbanisation can be seen on all the families of different castes. Similarly, rising rate of literacy, particularly among the younger age groups, has encouraged the village youth to take up jobs in areas other than agriculture, mostly in towns and cities.

These visible changes in village life suggest that today's village cannot be understood in terms of rural versus urban but as a part of the rural-urban continuum. During the 1950s and 1960s, a trend had already arisen when the village was first studied in the 1950s. The trend was visible, but now it is very apparent. A hint towards this trend was offered in the earlier book. Yet that study was moulded in the framework of ethnography.

In the 1950s, the village as a vertical unity provided the starting point for intensive study. Different castes in the village could be put in a ritual hierarchical order. In that system each caste was seen as a horizontal unity spread over a circle of villages, called *Chokhala*.

Since then the competitive character of each caste for finding its own social space began to be emphasised, and a situation in between the two was viewed as a caste could be treated as non-competitive strata. The last view appears to be nearer the situation prevailing in Ranawaton-ki-Sadri for the phase being recorded by the year 2004. Members of different castes have begun exploring avenues of their own development in the urban setting, enlarging their scope by working in other neighbouring villages. Still the village remaining as the key residential unit having basic connections with the land continues to maintain its own vitality along with extended work in neighbouring villages as well as urban centres. Such a situation can best be visualised through the manner in which members of different castes are based in the village and acquire additional skills to find a place in the expanding setup. These are presented for each of the castes in the village separately along with relevant points, with the Rajputs having been described earlier.

Gadri

Gadri constitute the group who were originally residents in the village. They have the largest number of family units, 55, which covers 26.69 per cent of household units in the village. Population-wise they constitute 19.46 per cent of the village residents and rank third among the various caste groups coming very close to the Rajputs with 28.5 per cent in the second place. Their highest position in the number of family units gives their family units a low average of membership of 4.1 members per unit, which for the village as a whole works out at 5.61. All the families belong to the *Duwala* clan and have at least 14 identifiable lineages with known parental connections have been treated as compounds in the present study. The residential pattern has provision for 33 *Nohras* with only three of them *pakka*, and they have only eight *pakka* houses as compared to 44 *kachha* ones.

The Gadri are traditionally associated with sheep-rearing; *Gadra* is the local term for the sheep. They are, however, connected with land in two ways: the irrigated 255 bighas and the non-irrigated 185, which work out to 4.64 bighas per family of the irrigated land, makes them the fourth highest landholding group among other castes of the village. If both types of land are counted together, the average comes to 8 bigha per family, which puts them on the third position. In their case even non-irrigated land has some meaning for animal grazing. For irrigation purposes they make use of the wells, and 51 of the families of the total of 55 have a share in the well. Three years of successive drought has rendered the wells almost dry. This had an effect also on the possession of cattle wealth. Most of the families sold out the sheep as only two of them could retain them. One of them is a two-person household with 1 bigha of land and uses 20 sheep as a major economic resource. The other one has 5 bighas of land, owns there buffaloes and three goats, and has a pair of bullocks and a plough. He has had education up to class 5 and is 35 years of age and lives with his wife and two children. In this case, he has a flock of 35 sheep, resides in a *kachha* house and has a cattle yard, which is also *kachha*. In this case sheep-rearing has been combined with agricultural and other pastoral activities.

On the score of human development the caste has made minor advancements In the 55 families, 21 have crossed the age of 50 and six of them were aged above 66. There are nine widows among these families, but it needs to be mentioned that widows are allowed to remarry if they are within the marriageable age. Education had a delayed start in this caste. Of the 220 persons, 151, that is, over two-thirds, 66.64 per cent, are illiterate. At the formal level 20 persons have received education, and 12 of them cleared the upper primary standard, with two of them going to the secondary stage. Even educational levels between classes 5 and 8 have prompted 10 members of the caste to go out for work in urban areas. Six of them work in the neighbouring town of Fateh Nagar as shop assistants ranging from grocer's shop to cloth-merchant and shoe store. One has learned carpentry work. Four young men have picked up other vocations: one sells ice cream in Ahmedabad and other works as a labourer in Mumbai. Indore has attracted two young men, one is a cleaner and the other a confectioner, *Halwai*. Within the village, the bicycle is the most popular conveyance with 48 households possessing it. Two persons have mopeds and one has a motorcycle, all used for personal commute. One family has shown some enterprise by acquiring a thrasher for obtaining com from the stalks. They make further use of the gadget by renting it to others.

The overall position of the Gadri in the village is which of a backward class that has been hit hard by successive droughts. There is marginal spread of education along with out-migration or continuation of residence in the village combined with jobs in the neighbouring town. Even the little education they have had has been sufficiently attractive to look for work in the urban areas. There is hardly any educated person above the age of 30 years and the average age of marriage is rather low.

Bhil

With 53 families in the village the Bhil have the second largest number of families, constituting a little over one-fourth of such units (25.73%) in the village. They have a strong tendency of setting up nuclear units, and their proportion in population is only one-fifth (20.85%). It appears that longevity of life is rather low as there are only two males and one female, who have crossed the age of 55 years. The number of males at 126 is slightly higher than that of the females. The average family size comes to 4.55 persons, which is lower than that of the village as a whole at 5.63 per cent.

The Bhil are the oldest residents of the village. Their main clan is *Mothi*, with six other clans together accounting for the remaining half. *Lalmata* is their principal deity with 31 families treating her as *Kuldevi*. *Bheruji* is also worshiped.

The average size of landholding among the Bhil comes to 2.28 bighas. Technically 79.75 per cent of their landholding are irrigated mainly through wells to which brothers have a joint share, but four years of continuous drought has disturbed their economy and 160 members of their families have sought some work as labourers and a little bit of support is obtained through the domestication of goats and hens. Families with a pair of bullocks and a plough have been able to go a little ahead with the acquisition of a bicycle for transport. This can be used also for going to work in the neighbouring town, and of the 53 families 22 have been able to acquire a bicycle. One of the persons got trained in ITI and became a worker in a thread factory, but the factory got closed. He now drives on a tempo for hire for transporting cargo and has a motorcycle and TV. He had 12 years of schooling, and along with his wife works on land, which is 9 bigha in size. He has a buffalo also. There is no child in the family. There is one more case of a person having a scooter for personal use. He along with his wife is classified as worker as he is landless, but he has a cow and a goat. He is a member of the Gram Panchayat. His cattle are covered under a special scheme which supports the supply of fodder and in case of those giving milk also with improved cattle feed. Most of the Bhil houses are *kachha*, and the few durables in the house are a metal water pot and a utensil.

The entire adult female population of the group is illiterate. Some effort in getting the new generation to school began lately. In August 2000, an Anganwadi scheme was launched in the village. In the fourth year of its working, 16 children got enrolled for the same. The pre-primary stage had some effect on the enrolment in the primary school that had started in July 1999, and by 2004 it had 15 boys and 7 girls on its rolls. The state primary school in the village had been raised to upper primary level in the year 2003–2004. The number of tribal children in that school for primary classes had risen to 33 with 14 boys and 19 girls. The slow start in education is clear from student population amount to just one boy and four girls in upper primary classes. As compared to the previous generation having few literate persons among the females, the Bhil now have 11 girls in the pre-primary stage and 26 in the primary, with 4 studying even higher classes. The changeover in one generation is striking. The possible factors leading to such a change are complex in nature; some of these may be mentioned. The location of Anganwadi in the former primary school building is within easy access. The programmes of the Anganwadi include a playful atmosphere for the children and the supply of mid-day snacks locally called *Ghugari*. A Sadhu woman prepares the same and loves doing this work for the children. A local lady from the upper group manages the Anganwadi, with it also used for taking timely care of the expectant mothers through the supply of nourishing tablets and other medical care. The programme of Pulse Polio also involves this institution. The tribal women and their children get actively associated with the Anganwadi; the mother and the children get used to a new way of life which is helpful in spreading the message of education and formal entry into the system. The Rajiv Gandhi Pathshala is also located in the southern part of the village within easy reach, and the institution which was set up on an experimental basis has now been regularised by making it a government primary school in July 2004. The village middle school got a new building in a more open space along the link road in the north-western direction of the habitation. The enrolment of 33 students in the primary section and five in the upper primary from among the tribal population suggests that the desire to acquire education has taken roots in the village and begun to reach the new generation. It needs to be mentioned that the mid-day meal scheme in this school continues to be applicable to all students in the primary classes, irrespective of caste and its relevance, and has gained greater acceptance among the members of this community. One can see a generational change taking place in the village, which is evident by the rise in the percentage of literacy of this group at 30 per cent.

Jat

The Jats are well-known cultivators. There are two major groups among them; the *Khaleri* had migrated from Ajmer region prior to the arrival of the Rajput, and the *Somarwal* who were invited from the neighbouring established village of *Patoliya* by the *Thakur* of the village to settle down as efficient cultivators promoting agriculture on the village lands. The first group lives in the centre of the village and the second in the extended village site on the north-eastern side where two compounds are important. The *Khaleri* constitute a group of related families, and it is from among them that the *Lambardar* of the village traditionally got appointed. His house is one where the *Heed* celebration (discussed in Chapter 5) takes place and then it moves towards the *Somarwal* section.

The presence of two *gotras* from two different regions permits them to have an occasional marriage connection within the village. The *Jats* prefer to call themselves *Patel*. The 19 families in the village have 34 males and 27 females indicating a slightly adverse sex ratio. The Jats occupy the third place among landowning groups in the village though their population ranks fourth. In terms of land available per family they top the list with an average size of 8 bighas, which is even ahead of the Rajputs for whom the figure works out to nearly 5 bighas of irrigated land. Of the 18 families, 11 have a pair of bullocks, and 15 families use well water for irrigation. As many as eight of them have two-wheelers, 11 use pump-sets, with one having even two pumpsets. There residential houses are spacious, and the number of *kachha* and *pakka* houses are distributed evenly. They are interested in having milch cattle; seven families have a cow, among whom two have two cows each; 13 families have buffaloes, and two of them have 4 buffaloes each, one 3, and 6 two each. Only six houses have separate cattle yard or *nohra*. This is partly explained by the large size of the inner courtyard of the house. Electricity is available with nine houses having an electric fan, five having radio and four TV connections. No family subscribes to a newspaper. Items like table and chair are rare with two families having the former and four the latter, and only one almira has been recorded in these families. For conveyance purposes, 11 have bicycles, and four have a motorcycle, and one, a scooter. The Jat families are low on having agricultural tools, which is a little surprising. Only five families have a plough and none has a tractor. So far as this village is concerned, Jat have been slow in making progress towards mechanisation of agriculture. In terms of diversification of occupation, one owns a tempo for passenger traffic in the twin settlements of the township of the Fatehnagar-Sanwad and the other a tempo for transporting goods. One of the persons having class 10 education works for the Hindustan Zinc Limited in the neighbouring town. It is of considerable interest that a boy with seven years of education runs a peripatetic refreshment stall in a four-wheeled trolley in Ahmedabad in Gujarat. Mumbai has attracted quite a few persons; six of them work in Mumbai, and all are aged below 35 years, with educational levels ranging from class 5 to 7. One of them works in a canteen, and his wife has joined him doing sewing work. Two brothers, 21 and 18 years of age, respectively, had education up to class 7 and work with a Seth and another youngster of same age group and educational level has got a job in a jewellery shop. Whereas one young man of 25 studied up to class 9 and he works in a grocery shop in the neighbouring town of Fateh Nagar; his younger brother, aged 22, studied up to class 8 and has moved to Mumbai to seek similar work.

The diversification in occupations among the new generation marks an orientation of the predominantly agricultural group towards the urban occupations. It is especially relevant here to note that only 10 persons in this caste have received middle-school level of education, and one of our perceptive informants from among the Rajput told us about a general tendency in the village among the middle-school-educated youth to move away from manual work; such a trend is not noticed in this caste as in the more agriculturally prosperous area of Haryana and western Uttar Pradesh where graduates and mechanised agriculture go together in rural areas.

Bairagi: Vaishnav

The Bairagi traditionally perform priestly functions and have acquired a new identity as the Vaishnav. Three generations ago, they had one family, which had two sons, and one of them in the next generation had one son and the other three sons. In this sense, they live in a compound. Their work requires some sort of literacy, and all the four elderly male members are literate; the eldest, aged 60, has out-migrated. His younger brother, aged 45, is literate and has 3 bighas of land, a cow and two buffaloes. He owns a tractor and a plough and rents out the tractor for agricultural work in the village and to manage this work he has appointed a Bhil as a driver. The house is *pakka* and also has the *nohra*, the place for the cattle. This was constructed in the year 2000. He has a TV at home and likes to watch news and religious serials

Vishnupuran, and the youngsters like programmes *Shaktimaan* and *Junior Zee* as well as movies songs. Among the household facilities available include a table and a chair and an almira. There is a fan and cooking gas. He has a cycle and a scooter and is a contractor. He got married in a village 65 kilometres away, and her daughter is married to a boy in Kailashpuri, a pilgrim centre 80 kilometres away. The daughter had received education up to BA second year. The son, aged 15, is studying in class 10 and looks after priestly duties on behalf of all the four families. He was observed performing 'pup' during a festival wearing a pant and shirt. The other brother, aged 25, studied up to class 8 and works in a photo studio in the neighbouring town. His wife hails from Udaipur and has passed class 7. His mother, aged 65, also lives with him as also elder brother's wife, who is widowed. Their services are used in running charitable *piaos* (water huts) on the bus stand and they are paid ₹ 300 per month during two-summer months. Her daughter, who is 10 years of age, is studying in class 6 and his son in class 3. Within the village they have only 3 bighas of non-irrigated land and have a cow and a calf. The family has a *kachha* house and a *nohra*. TV is used for watching programmes like *Chitrahaar* and *Rangoli*. There is a ceiling fan in the house and a cycle for transport.

The third brother, aged 35, is literate and has gone out for work. His wife is also literate and comes from a village 60 kilometres away. The son is studying in class 9, and the daughter, aged 13, studies in class 8. Three bighas of non-irrigated land needs help of others in cultivation. A transistor and a TV are available at home; elder family members like to watch the *Vishnupuran* and *Filmi Dhamaka*, combining both the sacred and the secular, as the youngsters like to watch *Junior Zee* and *Shaktimaan* and *Aryamaan*. A cycle and a scooter are available for transport, and there is an electric fan in the household.

The group is small in size and gets connected with others similarly placed at long distances, both for purposes of marriage and the *Chokhala*; the religious centre at Matrikundiya – 30 kilometres away – serves as a rallying point. Thus, the group has wider interconnections. One of the boys works in a voluntary agency in the tribal area, and one person has tried for employment in Gulf Countries. Another person, aged 40 and educated up to class 7, learnt tailoring; he had worked for a while in Kuwait where he did tailoring. Upon his return from Kuwait, he opened a small restaurant in Udaipur. Similarly, another Bairagi boy went to Muscat and took on carpentry work.

These families have rights of worship in the village temple. In terms of actual performance, the young boy with class 9 education has acquired enough ritualistic knowledge to perform the pujas (prayer rituals) efficiently and offers worship on behalf of all related families. In this sense, the ownership rights is separated, yet one person renders services in the traditional sector, as others seek non-traditional sources of employment outside the village and the country.

Daroga

The Daroga are said to be a caste consisting of children born to Rajput aristocracy through extramarital relations. These people were then hired by the Rajput elite as domestic servants. It is important to mention that these extramarital relations were managed with women of different service castes. When any Rajput was married, the family of his bride would gift him some maid servants. It is with these women that the Rajputs bore children and who were fed and settled. All such families were then designated *Daroga*.

It is important to record here that the Thakur of the village with a progressive outlook discontinued the practice and allotted land to the members of the Daroga group. There are three households of this group left in the village. One family head is 60 years old with a little literacy. His wife is illiterate and their 15-year-old son has nominal education; he studied up to class 3. They have just 1 bigha of non-irrigated land and one goat. All work as wage-labourers in the village. They have a *pakka* house and a cycle. The second family head is 45 years old and has received education up to class 8. His wife is illiterate, and they have three sons; the eldest one, 10 years of age, studies in class 5, and the second son grazes the cattle. The mother, 75 years of age, lives in the house and is a widow. With 1 bigha of land, a cow and a goat as resources the man acts like a log cutter in the village. The third unit is of a one-member household with a boy of 15 years living alone after the death of the grandfather, and after the demise of the parents there is no one to educate him; 1 bigha of irrigated land is all that he has. The three family units are just surviving in the village. One of the families is known to be using *Rawat* as a surname and has a tractor that is lent on hire, besides a motorcycle.

Kumhar

The Kumhar are traditionally potters. There are three families in the village. They belong to the common gotra *Haminga*, but have different grandfathers. One of the families is associated with village Sanwad; the man makes pots and visits the village once a week. His wife sells water-pots going door to door. Both of them are illiterate. They have 5 bighas of irrigated land and own one-third of a share in a well. The house is *kachha* but they have a music system which was on at the time of the enquiry. The first son is 29 years of age and has studies up to class 7 and is working in Mumbai. His wife is illiterate, but their daughter, 8 years of age, is in class 3. The second son is aged 21 years and has read up to class 10 in the neighbouring town; he is married and his wife, aged 19, has studied up to class 6 in a school 25 kilometres away from the village. Another son also works in a private company in Mumbai. He was at the village at the time of the enquiry and the wife living in her parental village was expected to join any time. The second household unit consists of two persons; the man of the family was 50 years of age and his wife 45. The man has weak eyesight but is able to turn the wheel. They have 4 bighas of irrigated land, a cow, and they live in a *kachha* house. The third household has four members. The man, aged 26, looks after the cultivation of 7 bighas of land, 2 of which are irrigated. They have a pair of bullocks and a plough and a buffalo and 2 goats. Irrigation is through a well. The house is *pakka* and the family has a cattle yard, *nohra*, *kachha*. He has a bicycle. The widowed mother, 45 years of age, looks after agricultural work. A daughter in the family, 10 years of age, is studying in class 3 in the village primary school. The man is literate. This family is not connected with the traditional work of pottery. The second family manages to do traditional work, and in the first family the second generation has gone out to Mumbai seeking jobs in private sector. A decline in preference for traditional work and search for alternatives in the urban region is visible in one case, and inclination towards taking up agriculture for sustenance in the other. On certain occasions of rituals, members of this group supply pots.

Suthar

The Suthar, the carpenters, are traditionally associated with manufacturing wooden articles required to meet productive as well as social and ritual needs of the villagers the way a Lohar (blacksmith) does. The function was earlier performed by a lone Lohar family and was subsequently taken up by Suthar with the out-migration of the former. There are four Lohar families in the village doing their traditional work and meeting the needs of local population, but with the out-migration of some members from the two families for better income the whole scenario has changed. While both continued to perform the work of carpenters, one Shri Jagannath, aged 30 and passed up to 8th class, moved to Muscat while another person, Shri Gopal Lal, aged 35 and studied up to class 8, opened a carpentry shop in the town of Fateh Nagar for better prospects. The acquisition of a two-wheeler proved handy and facilitated their out-migration while Gopal Lal purchased a scooter and used it for visiting Fateh Nagar in connection with his business. Jagannath, who had also worked in Muscat, helped him in procuring motorcycle, which he used for visiting the city market. The urban connections of half of the Suthar families helped create new demands of their services in the town while maintaining their links with the native village as well. The urban links brought sophistication in their traditional vocation also, which helped them in extending their trade linkages to urban markets as well.

Kalal (aka Jayaswal)

Kalal is a caste that is traditionally associated with sale of liquor, but they have moved to new occupations and now call themselves Jayaswal. Currently, there are five families in the village and four of them have a common ancestor. The eldest couple is 60 years old and has 3 bigha of irrigated land and a cow. Their house and cattle yard are *pakka* and there is a bicycle. The second son of the common ancestor have three sons, and they have found alternate income sources for themselves besides the traditional share of 3 to 4 bighas of irrigated land. One of these families is a two-person household. The man is educated up to class 7 and has set up a flourmill which is run by electricity. He lives in a *pakka* house and converted the *nohra* into a *pakka* construction in 2001. They have an electric fan, a TV and a cycle. The village has only two flourmills and running one of them is a major activity that brings the family in contact with the majority of the villagers. The second brother, 35 years of age, has received education up to class 8 and now works as a tailor in the village. His wife, aged 30, is illiterate and performs household work. Their only son has read up to class 8. With 4 bighas of irrigated land, two goats, and a well, he lives in a *kachha* house with a *kachha nohra*; we saw a table and a chair in the house. Other facilities of the household included a fan, a TV and a bicycle for transport. The third brother, 30 years of age, has read up to class 5 and is a truck driver for a Seth. His wife, aged 27, is illiterate and does household work. Of the two sons, the elder one is six years of age and studies in class 1. A part of the household is *pakka*, the *nohra* is *kachha*; the family owns a cow and has a share in the well. An electric fan and a TV as well as a transistor are available as comforts and they have a bicycle for transport.

The fifth family has not had any connection to the other four families over the past two generations but it carries the same gotra. The family head is 60 years of age, educated up to class 5; his wife has also received education up to class 4 and looks after household work. The man looks after agricultural work with 15 bighas of irrigated land and has an engine for use in irrigation, which has hardly been used as there was no water in the well for the last four years. His house is *pakka* with electricity connection; there are two fans, a TV and a radio. An important member of the family is the grandmother who is said to have crossed a hundred years in age. The two sons in the family with education up to class 7 and class 8, respectively, go to Fateh Nagar to work as shop assistants in a general merchandise shop.

Members of this caste have tried to look for improving their economy through non-agricultural work in the village and the neighbouring town and used their secondary level of education to good effect. They are no longer associated with the liquor business and as such are a good example of mobility and *Sanskritisation*.

A new migrant belonging to the Shaktawat branch of the Rajput has taken over liquor agency.

Keer

The Keers are traditionally associated with growing vegetables in river beds. Two brothers of the group sold out their land to someone in a neighbouring village, and six years ago they purchased the land belonging to the Maheshwari trader who had left for better business in

Gujarat. The Keer families are now based in the village and pursue urban occupations with one working at a jeweller's shop in Fateh Nagar, and the other left for Saudi Arabia extending the traditional work. The group is known to play the role of a keeper of a calf at the Gavri festival, adding to the comic scenes in the interlude. The caste is a new arrival in the village, as the Maheshwari represents the group that has left the village for good.

Teli

The two families of the Teli live at the north-western end or the entrance of the old settlement of the village. Both of them have oil-pressing units. One of them has a thrasher, which he lends on hire during harvesting of crops. His wife is a manual worker at the Ayurvedic dispensary, lives separately and looks after a small grocery shop. The two daughters are attending the primary classes in the village. The man looks after agriculture with 6 bighas of land and has a buffalo. His parents, aged 60 and 55 respectively, live with him. The head of the second family is a young man of 25 who had received education up to class 6 and he cultivates land held as common property. His brother goes to the town of Fateh Nagar for work as a shop assistant and has received education up to class 6. The widowed mother lives with him. The Rajput families pay special attention to this small group and have the tradition of looking after the food requirements on the occasion of a death in the family. The Teli families combine a multiplicity of activities in the traditional, agricultural and business sectors to run their households.

Khatik

The Khatik are traditionally associated with the sacrifice of the male goat at the altar holding the hind legs of the sacrificial animal which is cut by a Rajput young man with the sword. The *Khatiks*, thus, have a special place in the performance of rituals and later in skinning the sacrificed animal. The meat of the sacrificed animal is then distributed as *Prasad* among the devotees. The caste thereby got associated with an unclean work and were placed among the lower strata of the society. Their continuous association with the patrons widened their cognitive map in terms of progress on the material front and other urban contacts, and this has placed them almost next to the Rajput. From among their four families, three chose to go to Vadodara and one to Ahmedabad; the eldest of the three brothers works as a manual labourer carrying goods from one place to another, the second became a helper in a shop where goods were sold to ration-card holders, and two of his sons as also the third brother are selling tea and snacks like omelettes on a cart which is locally called *Lari* – an abrupt version of the word Lorry. Another elder went to Ahmedabad carrying on the same trade and his son has succeeded him. The elder person who had gone to Vadodara has returned home and at the age of 60 looks after the work of the rural household. He lives in a *pakka* house with electric connection and a telephone through which he maintains contacts with his three children now running their own *Lari* in Baroda, and he visits them once in two months or whenever he feels like. As many as six members of these families currently own such mobile teashops in the two large cities of Gujarat; had they tried this experiment in the neighbouring town where their caste could have been identified, the experiment could not have started. The social status of the caste would have come in the way. Migration to large urban centres has come in handy and sufficient income is getting generated to make *pakka* houses in the village and acquire telephone and other electric gadgets. Together, these families have ten two-wheelers, which includes scooters, mopeds and motorcycles; one of them is used by the third generation for going to school and the rest are used for personal transport. The first generation of migrants had education up to class 5 and the second generation up to class 8. With nine families combined, share of landholdings comes to 31 bigha of irrigated land and 2 bigha of non-irrigated land; with the average coming to 3.44 bighas it puts them at seventh rank among different castes, next only to Jatiya (3.90). Both of these castes socially belong to the category of the Scheduled Castes, but in terms of their development the *Khatik* are a special case.

The land records of the village cover 15 units among the Khatik, of whom five have more than 1 hectare of land each, with another one touching almost 1 hectare, 0.98 hectare to be precise. Others have smaller landholdings. Four households live in *kachha* houses, which reflects their lower standard of living. Only one head of the family among them is literate, yet their children are going in for education with the eldest who studied up to class 8 and another who completed class 12 and trying to get some technical training; in that sense this community is markedly different from other Scheduled Castes. The Caste group as a whole has a fair proportion of elders, as persons in the age group of 60 and above head six of the nine households. The Khatik thus represent a special case of a Scheduled Caste having two groups, the higher one through urban exposure, improving its status in the village, and the lower one opting for traditional work and thus continue to remain poor but taking initiatives nevertheless for the educational development of the second generation.

Kharol

The Kharol are a group traditionally associated with making salt; a small heap of mud outside the village reminds one of that activity, which is no longer pursued. There are only two families of this caste in the village. They had the same grandfather and now have 4 bighas of land each. The well is held in common and cultivation is their main source of livelihood. The elder family head is illiterate as also his first son. The second son, 12 years old, is studying in class 4 in the village. Two young daughters, aged 9 and 7, respectively, are also studying in the village school. They live in a *kachha* house but have a pair of bullocks and a plough. One buffalo and three goats complete the family's cattle wealth. A bicycle as means of transport is also available. The second family has a young man of 22 years as the eldest male member, who has studied up to class 8. His mother and grandfather also live with them, both widowed, with the grandfather aged above 70 years. The young man is married, and the couple has a daughter who is one-and-a-half year old. Besides agricultural land, they have two cows, one calf and a goat; their house is *kachha*, but the family has an electric fan and a cycle. The common family deity is *Khodaji*.

Jatiya (earlier known as Chamar)

The Jatiya is the new designation adopted by the group that was earlier called the Chamar, two generations ago.

There are 11 families in the village. The oldest couple are 65 and 60 years of age, and one more at 55 and 50 who can be counted among the old; the couple aged 50 and 45 years of age occupy the third position. In all other cases oldest males are aged below 50 years. All the families above the age of 25 are illiterate. Among the males, only one person in the adult group, 35 years old, had education up to class 5. In the next generation, some traces of education are visible among the boys; one aged 15 could reach class 7 and he has been engaged, and other one, 10 years old, has done schooling up to class 2 and joined work in a hotel in Surat (Gujarat). Boys and girls below the age of 7 have decided to attend the school. The Jatiya have small plots of land varying from 2 to 5 bighas; occasionally they do possess some small animals. The majority of the families have only a bicycle as a means of mobility. They are cultivators in the village and also do other kinds of labour; in addition, one of these has joined a factory in Surat.

An effort was made to set up a housing colony for the members of this group through state assistance on the southern side of the village habitation. They moved to the new site, but they felt it a disturbed locality, feeling that ghost and evil spirits pervade the locality; all but two families left the locality and returned to their original house or other areas in the company of other villagers. This is the second time that a group experiment in migration has failed. The earlier effort that was made two generations ago to move towards the Tehsil Headquarters had met a similar fate. Of the 11 families, only two live in *pakka* house. This caste group is no longer associated with leatherwork but takes up construction work or engage in seasonal agricultural labour.

For curing the hide, a migrant *Regar* worker has been invited by the village head to settle down in the village.

Rural-urban connections now form an integral part of the life of villagers, a phenomenon visible across all caste groups but in varying degrees. The Rajputs lead the village both in moving out for work and bringing in urbanising effects to strengthen their position. The *Khatik* through urban activities have followed next. In both castes two strata are visible. The Sadhu now basically look for out-migration as do the *Suthar*. The Teli have responded positively to urbanising influence. The case of the Bhil and the *Jatiya* continues to cause some concern as their standards of living are low and their age composition is indicative of a tapering-off at the higher levels. The Jat remain agricultural. The *Gadri* are somewhat handicapped when it comes to facing droughts. The dearth of grass as fodder for their sheep and goats in times of drought is regarded as visitation of the wrath of gods. Yet new upward trends in the communities seeking educational development are visible at all levels, and middle-school-level attainments do promote a tendency to go to urban regions for jobs.

5

Rituals of the Village Life

A Selective Study

The ritual structure of village formed part of detailed description and analysis in the first edition of A *Rajasthan Village* (1967). In the present restudy, the few events of the rituals of the life cycle that took place during the course of the enquiry have been noted. The manner in which the tradition is continued and innovations introduced forms a part of the material presented here. The festival of *Govardhan Puja* on the day next to *Dewali* has received attention in village studies in India with McKim Marriott (1955) using the illustration for conceptualising the interplay between the great and the little traditions in the form of parochialisation. Alternate meanings and significance of Govardhan Puja are provided, and the complex of playful rituals along with the cattle wealth is also discussed. A combination of folklore with rituals /ceremonies/events gives them an overall or gestalt-like character. Differential participation of groups and their contribution to the communitarian aspects of rural life are clarified. The complex of rituals interconnecting the tribal life, its folklore and its integration with the classical festival of *Jal Jhulni Ekadashi* at the initiative of the local village chief are given a special focus in this chapter.

Rituals of the Life Cycle

Death

Rituals immediately following the events of marriage and death in the Rajput families were observed during the course of our study. The events become significant both for the maintenance of the norms and a few departures therefrom. The case of death relates to the mother of the *Vakil Sahib* (lawyer). According to the norms, the younger brother had carried ashes for immersion at *Hardwar*. On return, an interrelated celebration was held to celebrate the return from the river *Ganga*. The state law does not formally allow the post-funeral dinners. People have developed a functional alternative in the form of the worship of the *Ganga Yatra* being celebrated along with other rituals. The prescribed period of mourning is observed; a white turban is worn, and other customs include head tonsure, and, the donning of new turban signifies the ritual of succession. The mourning comes to an end with dinner on a large scale; all the kinsmen are notified through letters. In a traditional manner, it was the function of the *Nai* to circulate the information, but these days postal services are used for this purpose. A new practice in urban areas has been added that include a photograph of the deceased along with the information. This practice is disliked by the villagers as they say that such a letter may ultimately be destroyed and find its way into the garbage thereby dishonouring the memory of the person's photograph. With this interpretation they reject this part of the innovation.

The dinner is served to a large number of people usually in the afternoon to facilitate the return of the guests to their villages before evening. The large number of guests are provided seats according to custom; guests are seated on the roof and castes of category I are also served there. Castes of category II are seated on one side on the floor and the category III on other side of the floor. In arranging this function the space of the 'compound' is used. After the completion of ceremony, mourning period comes to an end and normal routine of life gets started.

In this case, earlier celebrations are recalled. Some deviations are talked about, but a few are purposely asserted. The village had taken a lead in changing the menu for the dinner a few years earlier. No sweet dishes are prepared, and the new practice is followed in this case, the occasion being interpreted as not one of feasting but a solemn occasion of paying respects to the departed soul. The Rajputs of the village took this initiative and considered themselves different from others in this context, thereby redefining their inter-village connections.

Marriage

A marriage among the Rajput family that has moved away from the *Rawala* and living in 'navi jagah' (new place) gets celebrated on a modest scale. Wedding ceremonies are held at the bride's place, and the marriage party travels by bus and returns the next day. An important detail that needs be mentioned is the part taken by the bridegroom to being more or less the key figure in arranging for the economy of the household and meeting the entire cost on his own. Earlier he had played the same role in the case of his sister's marriage and had not bothered other members from the family to contribute to these costs on this count. These marriages indicate the manner a self-made man redefines the obligations in a marriage, which others would not like to treat as a representative case. The person concerned, however, retains his self-defined position thereby confirming that the norms and the variations as well as the events themselves need closer observation for understanding the process of even rituals of the lifecycle and their differential meaning and impact for the actors in a community.

Remarriages

Over three-fourth of caste groups in the village permit widow remarriage or even second marriage for both men and women. The first marriage can be terminated and remarriage, locally called *Nata*, is arranged. During the last two years, a few cases were reported. In the Jat caste, a person had married a woman who had primary education, could run the sewing machine, but was not good at preparing meals. The man felt uneasy and could take food only out of compulsion. He divorced the woman and brought in another woman who could also sew clothes and prepare delicious food. Normally such marriages create tensions and claims on the ornaments. In this case the man got ornaments worth ₹ 75,000 given for the second wife. These matters are settled through the *Jati-Panchayat* with the help of a few leading members of the villages concerned.

The case of remarriage of a Jat girl took 10 years to be solved. Bhagwani, daughter of Kalu, got married to Premchandra of village Ladhana in Mavli Tehsil according to the traditions of the caste. This event is significant for the reason that the matter was referred to the judiciary, and the court of the Upper District Judge Chittorgarh delivered the judgment on 12 October 2001. The case was tried under Section 13 of the Hindu Marriage Act for divorce. It is recorded that the marriage had taken place about 10 years earlier (5 March 1991). The husband stated that he had gone to wife's residence several times to bring her to his home but she came only on three occasions, stayed for 5 or 10 days and went back to her parental house on her own. The husband's plea was that he was still willing to take the wife, but her father was unwilling to send her. It was mentioned that the father had earlier given the wife's younger sister in her second marriage *Nata*, and earned quite some money, and that he wanted to do the same again. In the proceedings statements of Bhagwani, her father, another *Jat* and a *Gadri* were recorded from one side, and those of the husband and four others from the other side. The court ruled that the husband had not taken care of the wife for a period exceeding two years and that she was entitled to get the divorce. It was also mentioned from the wife's side in the proceedings that they were childless; there was a claim for return of things given in the dowry amounting to ₹ 20,000 that the husband's party had kept for himself but the court rejected this plea. The court further ruled that Bhagwani was entitled to receive ₹ 500 per month towards meeting maintenance cost from the date of the judgment till she gets remarried. The judgment was delivered on 12 October 2001. After the death of the father, the girl was taken care of by her mother and her brother. The latter played an active role in getting her remarried in the *Nata* form in July 2004. The new husband got a set of ornaments prepared making them available to the wife.

The case is important because the settlement in a traditional dispute had been formally referred to the judiciary, and after obtaining the verdict the concerned parties took their own actions again according to customs prevalent in the caste. Here again the role of the brother and brother-in-law of the second sister had become important.

Festivals in the Village

Govardhan Puja and Khekhra

Festivals have their own cycle. They connect local rituals with classical patterns and lend a regional colour to the same. *Dewali* is known as a series of events connected with the goddess of wealth. In the peasant society agricultural wealth is important, and the day next to Dewali is observed as *Khekhra*, which in the morning takes the form of *Govardhan Puja*. The classical version relates to the story of *Govardhan Parvat*, the story of Indra getting angry and pouring rains, and Lord Krishna comes to the rescue of the villagers by holding the mountain on one finger of the hand and gives shelter and protection to the peasants and cattle. The regional variation considers Govardhan as the name of a Gujar who is remembered on this occasion. In the case of Kishangarhi, Marriott (1955) had split *Govardhan* into *Gobar* + *Dhan* translating it as cow dung wealth. In the region under study Govardhan gets a human touch and worshipped as an ancestor for a key human figure of some importance. The occasion brings together a number of functionaries' folk songs and a series of events that accompany the same.

From the neighbouring village of Patoliya, the Bhil come in a group singing the devotional lines recalling various lords and deities, and the names are recalled; the *Heed* in a running translation in English is recited in the following manner:

> Which god to respect first and whose name to be taken? Let us remember Mata Saraswati, Ganpati and invoke them. The founding deity of the village Chamunda Mata.
>
> The name of *Lal Bai Rani, Joheda Thakur* who protects the animal wealth.

After every two lines the refrain *'heed-hai bhai'* follows. The name of the deity appears in the first half of the line and then her qualities. In this case, *Lal Mata* is mentioned as *Lal Bai Rani*, conferring upon her the glory of secular power as well. Then follow Charana Thakur's name associated with curing the dog bite. This is a place in Rail Magra Tehsil towards the north. References are also made to Bhamrasiya Thakur where cases of snakebite are cured, then follows an admission of mistakes or forgetfulness in invoking proper name with generalised statement about 9,00,000 gods. With these introductory remembrances, the song returns to the main theme as follows:

> Gokul, where Krishna was born, in Mathura, the Gujar girls over the green hills. Let the bullocks be decorated and offered Aarti on a decorated plate.
>
> Krishna peeped through a hiding place and the cows got disturbed running about in all directions. Their attendant Govardhan lost presence of mind and died in the stampede.

From then on Govardhan Gujar began to be worshipped and his name became everlasting. The collective hymn recited by the Bhil of the neighbouring village perpetuates the story behind the worship of Govardhan Gujar puts him in the company of the deities to be remembered as well as to the centres associated with the protection and cure from the little dangers prevalent in the region. The *'Heed'* begins with two classical deities, *Sharda* and *Ganpati*, and then comes to the deity of the village and that of the Bhil; references are made to three regional deities and generalised plurality by just referring to the number 9 lakh (9,00,000). After establishing these confidence-building measures come the references to Krishna, the sacrifice of Govardhan and his immortalisation. At the cultural level this represents the phase of incorporation of local and regional elements into a classical frame, whereas Marriott had described it merely as parochialisation (1955). In this case, folk songs have been merged with classical music. This is a good example of a creative venture, a queer mixing of the twin processes of parochialisation and universalisation, followed by practices associated with the worship.

The Bhil women collect cow dung and prepare the image of Govardhan before the houses in the village for which they receive gifts of some grains. Around 9 am in the morning, village women go around their neighbourhoods to collect cow dung and worship Govardhan. A few drops of water are sprinkled over it symbolising its holy bath. Coloured thread is placed and offer of curd follows. The next step is fixing the upper portion of sugar cane with leaves and cotton pieces on the sticks. A lamp containing ghee is lighted along with the essence. Nearby, a circular area is marked by cow dung in a liquid form and rod is used for mixing curd. The women paint some figures there that symbolise the churning process. This part of the function conclude with the *Aarti* and some presentations to Govardhan.

Collective Activities Connected with the Worship of the Oxen

The time for the afternoon or evening functions is settled according to the *Muhurt* fixed by the Pandit. The bullocks are bathed during the day and decorated with colourful paintings or signs; the horns are coloured with two or three paints and made attractive for the purpose by garlands, peacock feathers and small balloons; a leather belt fixed with jingle bells tied on it made in the form of a garland is placed around neck.

The village *Balai* marks the boundary with the line being marked by cow dung mixed with water and the place assigned for the bullocks of every family in the village. The Balai goes around the village inviting people along with their bullocks to come to the place in front of the *Rawla*. As the people collect together the *Dholi* begins beating the drum and proceedings start with the *Kumhar* bringing the earthen pot or *Kalash*. The *Nai* brings the plate containing items of worship from inside the house of the village Thakur. The Pandit recites the mantras as the *Kalash* is placed outside the main gate. The *Thakur* of the village performs the puja as directed by the priest seeking welfare of the entire cattle wealth of the village, and then the *Lambardar* of the village offers sweets to the bullocks from the plate brought earlier by the *Nai* from the *Rawla*. The Patel offers ghee and lamp lighted on an earthen base with one hand and takes aside the rope used in preparing buttermilk in the other hand and gently strikes the same on the bullocks. They move a little backwards and get excited as the *Dholi* beats the drum louder and louder, and the children burst crackers. The bullocks run hither and thither as their bells begin to jingle and the bell sounds fill the atmosphere. The attendants run along with the bullocks and carry them to their destination. These ceremonies last 10–15 minutes. The *Kalash* is taken back to the *Rawla* and the grain on which it had been placed is collected by the *Dholi* who distributes it to various actors in the rituals. On the village Thakur's behalf, the *Nai*, *Kumhar*, *Dholi*, and *Balai* receive a gift of grains and articles for food and the Pandit is offered grains for his services.

The ceremony is conducted once again in front of the house of the *Patel* where articles for the puja and gifts for the participating actors are given on the behalf of Patel. The ceremony is conducted outside the house of the *Lambardar* with further performance, and the same performance is repeated once again at the place outside the house of Narayan Jat of the *Khaleri* lineage. The last performance was scheduled to be held at Narayan Gadri's place. However, it has not been done for the last three years. The ceremony is referred to as teasing the bulls (*bail bhadkana*). With the increasing mechanisation of agricultural operations and the consequent reduction in the number of oxen, the oxen population has gone down a little with only four pairs at the Rawla, nine at the Patel, five at the *Lambardar* and six at Narayan Jat's outer space of the residence earmarked in liquid cow dung. In all the houses, sweets are prepared for the evening and consumed as part of the dinner. Lamps are lighted in the evening in the houses, including both the sides of the main gate.

The definition of the cattle wealth includes smaller animals like sheep and goats; they are also given bath and colours are applied particularly to the sheep. People use different colours that later become identification marks for the flock owner. With the rise of auto vehicles as mechanised sources of transport, the old method of giving special recognition to the animals used in transport is extended to the inanimate sector and one sees marks of worship on them as well. This, however, is a private affair for the owners. The nature of festivals serving as connecting links of rural economy with rituals is carried over to the organised sector of rural life signifying their continuity in the changing situation. The festivals act as rituals of transition from one season to another as well as that of welcoming new crops to become a part of change in daily consumption. The village does not have a full contingent of different caste groups and welcomes specialised groups that offer help during the rituals. In the present case, the priest (*Pandit*) and the drummer (*Dholi*) and a group of the tribals also come from the neighbouring village to complement the human resources needed for the performance of different connected actions.

On the eleventh day after Diwali, a few lamps are lit to mark the commencement of auspicious moments connected with renewing important events and rituals like marriage; the day marks the rise of gods from the slumber lasting nearly four months. In popular version, this is called *Lodi Diwali* or the minor *Diwali* and in its Sanskritised form, it is called *Dev Uthaoni*.

Whereas most of the places of worship continue to be taken care of, one sees the rise and decline of a few such centres. The platform of the *Lal Mata* has been renovated, a new *Shiva* temple has come up in the village in an attractively painted style, and a new centre of *Khandoliya Bawji* has come up which has special significance even for those who seek supernatural blessings for various elections, besides other remedies. Located among the fields on the eastern side adjoining four villages, the place is attracting devotees coming from locations as far as 60 kilometres away from the village. In the village on the banks of the tank, a block of bricks are placed to provide elevation over a platform built for *Radaji*. A few centres suffered from the loss of charismatic power on the social organisational side. The *Bhil Bhopa* (priest) at Anjankheda, Gulab Naik, was reputed for identifying and resolving problems of the people, and could say that in poetic compositions, then speak on behalf of the deity becoming 'I', and state 'I know and would correct this.' On his death, his attendant Onkar Bhil succeeded him, but he performed the trance in village Sadri near his residence. Knowledgeable informants say that the successor had only half the efficacy of the original; then the third person in line of succession got reduced it to one-tenth and eventually the charisma faded out. Smaller places of worship have the *Bhopa* as the priest, the *Hajuriya* as a deputy, and a few attendants belong to the non-hierarchical order. The Sadhus of the village call themselves *Vaishnav* and worship the temple in the central part of the village. All the male members in the four families take turn among themselves to perform priestly duties, but they have also found one youngster who can perform *Puja* on behalf of all the four houses; what offerings they get from devotees are distributed proportionately and the priest who performs the Puja gets his share for the duties performed.

Gavri and Jal Jhulni Ekadashi

Jal Jhulni Ekadashi is celebrated on the 11th day of the second fortnight of the month of *Bhadrapad*; the celebration marks Lord Krishna's first outing after His birth to go to banks of the river Yamuna and play. At the regional levels important centres like Charbhuja in Rajsamand district and Sanwaliya Ji in Chittorgarh district attract lots of devotees. The images of the deity are carried in procession to several temples in various towns and cities. In the afternoon, the deity is placed in a *viman* or improvised decorated seat and carried on the shoulders usually by the youth. In the village under study, a complex of rituals have been added to the festival, which acquires a communitarian character.

The village has a significant proportion, nearly one fourth, of the population of the tribals, the Bhil. At this time of the year the *Bhil* in the Mewar region observe *Gavri* festival. It is celebrated over 40 days by a group of Bhil performers who combine religious abstinence for the duration and enact dance drama festival during the day at designated places. The tradition is that after marriage, members of the parental village of the girl get involved in the organisation of the event. The tradition is called 'taking the *Gavri*'. While the village has a sizable *Bhil* population, its location in the region is more in the area where the tribals are a minority. As such, they are on the periphery of the tribal area, and it is difficult for them to accept the responsibilities of organising such a venture. During his tenure as *Thakur* in the village, Ram Singh introduced an innovative measure by suggesting that the *Bhil* in the village perform the dance drama events on *Jal Jhulni Ekadashi*, and the following day the performers are freed from the strict discipline of abstinence from liquor or any such indulgence. The combination of a part of the tribal tradition with the classical festival and its legitimation by the village chief characterised the peculiar combination of the sacred text, folklore and local authority.

The dance drama begins in the afternoon in front of the village temple where the viman for the deity is built. The participants in the *Gavri* festival come from among the *Bhil* population only. The festival is witnessed by members of all the groups in the village, with women and children watching the same with considerable interest. After invoking the deities, the proceedings turn to secular dimensions as the drama is performed based on two inter-related stories.

Two important groups are formed; one of the *Banjara*, the other of the *Meena*. The scene was traced back to the period when means of communications were few, and the *Banjara* were the carriers of merchandise. They would pack the material in huge bags, load them on the bullocks, and they always went together as a group. They would cover hills and valleys en route trade centres. Such movements were risky, and they could be way laid crossing difficult terrains through the hills. The local tribals controlled the area and would ask for a sort of ransom or *Chauki* of one rupee. The traders objected to such a payment and the *Meena chowkidars* start beating them. The former also carry the *Bhala* (spear). The dance drama goes on for a few minutes. The Meena wear a crown made of leaves of Neem tree on their heads and keep on dancing and raiding the Banjara. The dance and the fight attract the audience. There are a few intervals, and the proceedings begin again by invoking the deity. At the next stage, one of the expert tribal actors takes up a sword and begins waving it with great speed during the dance. He is recognised by the audience as a skilled performer who is slightly handicapped in the sense that he has a failing eyesight. In the struggle enacted in the drama, one of the *Meenas* is killed by the *Banjara*; this enrages the entire tribal community as they jump upon the procession and *Banjara* lose their goods in the process. An elderly visitor explains that all this came about for refusing to pay just one rupee demanded by the *Meena* as their toll tax in the informal sector.

The story goes to the next act when a *Banjarin*, that is, a person dressed in female clothes, enters the scene during the travel; the lady takes leave of the party on some pretext like going to a village for getting some milk. The party keeps on moving and the *Banjarin* is left out of the party, or taken as lost for her non-appearance, and the party moves on. At an appropriate moment, a new *Banjarin* is substituted. The audience is aware of these stories and can easily understand the theme of the dance drama and keep entertaining themselves accordingly. No separate stage is set up. The entire scene is performed on an open space in front of the temple with the audience taking vantage positions around the circle.

They are aware of the sequence of events, the alternate invoking of the deity and the enactment of the scenes, and as the last scene concludes all the visitors suddenly rise up in full knowledge that the programme has been concluded. Even the school students join the spectators, and for practical reasons a half-day holiday is allowed. A few of the *Bhil* students also take part as actors in the programme. On the first day in the year 2004 the proceedings were halted one hour earlier on getting the news of the death of a *Bhil* in the village.

The sacred part of the *Jal Jhulni Ekadashi* starts immediately on conclusion of the *Gavri*. The *Sadhu*, now called *Vaishnav*, plays the leading role and decorates the viman for placing the deity on it. It is a small canopy-like structure with the curtains forming the little enclosure around the deity on three sides and the top. Parallel wooden rods are tied to the structure in such a way at both ends, the front and the back, that three and four young men from either side can lift it on their shoulders. As soon as it is carried out of the temple and brought to the streets, a few women offer coconut, bend down and pass under the viman from the front side to the back. This is indicative of the respect and salutations given to the deity. The procession moves along the street and turns towards the village tank where the deity is placed on the bank and the *Pujari* bathes the deity; he brings it back to the *viman* and prepares it for other parts of the worship. Meanwhile, everyone, young and old, also takes a bath in the pond. This activity in 2004 became colourful; the tank was filled with water through timely rains after a gap of six years. Meanwhile, the Jat elderly woman *Chandi Bhua* lent her help in peeling off the coconuts, making small pieces of about a centimetre wide of the main fruit, which would later form part of the *Prasad*. The *Pujari* performed the *Aarti*, as others beat the circular plate adding to the devotional atmosphere. Some people sang songs on the occasion as the sacred water in the form of Prasad began to be distributed followed by as spoon full of powdered coriander leaves. The small pieces of coconut fruit also were distributed; the whole atmosphere was filled with slogans praising the glory of Lord Krishna; the return journey commenced before the sunset. The procession is carried to the *Rawala* and a few *Rajput* houses to enable the women in their family to have *Darshan* and offer a few gifts. The ceremony is concluded with the return of the procession to the temple. Whereas the women of the Rajput group get the opportunity to participate in the festival in their own compounds, women of other groups pay their respects outside the temple or while taking part in the procession moving to the tank. The communitarian nature of the festival is quite visible with the involvement of various groups cutting across caste lines and participation of women collectively from most of the castes, with special arrangement for women of higher castes to receive the deity in their compounds, make offerings of coconut, and redistribute Prasad among their own group.

6

New Institutions

As new institutions in the wake of extending welfare activities enter a village community, they get into either a hospitable climate or a hostile climate, which varies from from place to place. Ranawaton-ki-Sadri belongs to the first category, as the traditional units in the social structure not merely create conditions for facilitating the arrival of new institutions but even initiate action to make them a part of rural life in a dignified manner. The interplay between modernising forces and traditional units forms the thrust of the approach to encompass each of the new institutions becoming a part of rural life, which happened during the first four years of the twenty-first century.

The Village School

The village school has undergone three phases of development:

1. As a small unit working within the village habitation in private and acquired buildings.
2. Construction of the school building outside the habitation as a government girls school.
3. Elevation of school's status to a government middle school that is open to boys as well.

In the first phase, the role of the village community was prominent in providing space for the school. For some time even a teacher was informally hired, and later a full-time government teacher joined the school.

In the second phase, the school was shifted outside the village habitation to its own premises. The only way in which the new facility could be obtained was by proposing it as a primary school for the girls. The initiative in this matter was taken by a young Sarpanch of the village, Sangram Singh, and the local MLA (Member of Legislative Assembly), Shyama Kumari Sengar.

In the third phase, the primary school was upgraded as government middle school, and the main initiative in this regard was taken by the lady Sarpanch, Anand Kanwar, the Panchayat Samiti member. Advocate Roop Singh, the Chairman of District Board, and the MP (Member of Parliament), Shri Chand Kriplani, besides the school headmaster, Bhanwar Singh.

1. In the pre-Independence period the villagers contributed ₹ 2 per student and hired a teacher from Patoliya to conduct classes in a Jat household. By 1952, with the establishment of the village Panchayat, a single-teacher school came into being in the same/adjacent place. The author had organised two study camps of graduate students of Maharana Bhopal College, Udaipur, which included recreational programmes in the evenings; an appeal was made to collect funds and contributions to support the programme. A tailor's family in the village moved out to the town and sold its house, which was purchased for the school at ₹ 800; the Rajput contributed half the amount.

2. In 1979, the village school was promoted to the status of the government girls upper primary school. Three new rooms were constructed, and a year later a meeting hall was added along with additional work carried to enhance the appearance, such as polishing of doors, and the village school was changed to a co-ed school to provide education to boys as well. Till then teachers used to come from outside the village during the school hours and returned to their places thereafter. The school was upgraded to the boys' school. Bhanwar Singh Ranawat, the headmaster, was transferred from *Patoliya* to this school; he is a resident of this village. There were a total of seven staff members, of whom two are from this village.

Initiatives in further development in the school came about during the period when Anand Kunwar Ranawat became the *Sarpanch* (February 1995 to 2000). Advocate Roop Singh Ranawat from the village had become a member of the *Panchayat Samiti* and played a key role in getting official sanctions and the budget. There were seven rooms in all and a veranda; a proper entry gate was added, which gave a new look to the school. The school organised games and sports events at the *Panchayat Samiti* level for three days in August 2001. Altogether 18 teams participated, and the villagers provided facilities for boarding and lodging. This was considered as one of the best tournaments organised in the district, and the occasion was used for announcing a grant of ₹ 50,000 for the construction of a prayer hall of 50' x 30' size. Advocate Roop Singh prevailed upon the members of the *Panchayat Samiti* and the MPs to increase the share to the tune of ₹ 2.40 lakh for the construction of the hall; the construction was completed in January 2004.

The headmaster of the school took initiative in getting grants from other sources to construct a water tank and funds for repairing and giving a face lift to the school building by painting it in pink shade. Appeals were made for getting recreational facilities like the swing and slippery. Sixty trees along with tree guards now form a part of the campus. The village Panchayat has allotted 1.5 bigha land and additional space of 3 *bigha* for playfields at the southern side of the village. The resources organised for the development of the school thus include funds from MPs' development schemes, the Lok Jumbish as part of *Sarva Shiksha Abhiyan*, the village *Panchayat*, and the state education department, besides voluntary contributions.

The school has at present a strength of 194 students, 94 boys and 100 girls for the academic year 2003–2004. Their demographic distribution is well-spread among different groups: 38 in the tribal category, 42 from Scheduled Castes (SCs), 85 Other Backward Classes (OBCs), and 29 in the general category. The school maintains a list of those who have secured top positions, and these are also well spread out among different social groups. Of special significance was a student from among the Scheduled Tribes (STs) who had obtained 14th rank in the district in class 8 and had passed class 11 in 2004 from the Fateh Nagar School. He had been encouraged personally by the headmaster of the school. The school gives the look of a vibrant institution.

The middle school provides education up to class 8. It had 15 students in the final class in 2001–2002 academic year, of whom 6 cleared the examinations in first division, 4 in second, 3 in the third, and 1 got supplementary but failed. Four girls completed their study and got married, and 5 students continued their studies and were studying in class 10 in schools in Fatehnagar, Patoliya and Sanvad. Among those who cleared in the first division, one got married and four continued their studies further.

For the academic year 2002–2003, of the 13 students who took examinations for class 8, two cleared in the first division; one girl did not study further and began tailoring work at home, and the other took admission to class 9 in the government higher secondary school in Patoliya; two students got supplementary, of whom the girl passed class 8 and got married, but the boy failed. Eight students cleared the examination in second division and six of them opted for further schooling in neighbouring towns such as Kakarwa, Patoliya and Fatehnagar; one boy has gone to Surat for work.

For the academic year 2003–2004, 14 students took the examination and three were unsuccessful. One girl cleared in the third division, one boy in the second division and seven in the first division. Thus, ten students of this batch are continuing their studies for class 9 at the three centres mentioned earlier. The above figures suggest a qualitative improvement in performance and a trend for continuing education, even though students went to three different centres. Of special interest is a Bhil student who cleared class 8 in first division and who had been encouraged personally by the headmaster of school for further studies in Fateh Nagar, and a girl student had secured a good rank in the district in 2004.

Educational efforts in the village continued to spread. In the newly settled area of the village to the south of the nucleus, the school named Rajiv Gandhi Swarna Jayanti

Pathshala was started in the year 1999, which by 2004 had five classes with 16 boys and 14 girls. The school started under a tree, but later a building with two rooms and an office was constructed under the same scheme. An SC teacher from the neighbouring village, which is also the village Panchayat centre, has been appointed and has undergone teachers' training. The institution has been raised to the status of a primary school along with three others in the *Panchayat Samiti*. Its location is in the area where SC population is concentrated. It has seven students from the SCs, all girls and 22 from the ST community; in this group there were seven girls and one boy from OBC. This serves the needs of the special categories of society.

The *Lok Jumbish* is a voluntary organisation and helps improve the standard of school buildings and other connected activities. It conducts surveys of non-school-going children and provides help in encouraging them to attend schools. Some training camps for teachers are organised: in summer vacation, the workers come for the block headquarters and are provided space in one of the outhouses of a teacher's family. The scheme has since been made a part of the Sarva Shiksha Abhiyan in the State of Rajasthan.

Health and education get combined in the activities of Anganwadi which is located in the former primary school with 30 boys and 29 girls. Community-wise distribution of students is as follows: 9 from SCs, 16 from STs (Bhil) and 34 from OBC. Here again, the institution happens to cater to the needs of special categories. It has been established in August 2000 and looks after the distribution of nutritious food to the pregnant and lactating women and children. It spreads knowledge about health practices and looks after small children, making them learn and play together.

Medical Facilities

An Ayurvedic health centre was established in 1975 in the residence of the village Sarpanch; within three years, two rooms and a covered veranda were provided through local contributions and handed over to the state Ayurvedic department. There is one physician and a compounder on full-time duty and a part-time peon. Dr Savitri Devi was the first physician to work there and Gita Devi, a nurse who retired from the village. Thus, the health centre was totally looked after initially by women, and this helped in making them acceptable to all. On their retirement, a few other persons came but left after a short tenure. In October 2001 Dr Laxmi Nand Sharma was transferred to this village. He lives in Udaipur city and commutes between the city and the village every day.

Earlier he had worked for a decade in a neighbouring large village Akola, and patients from there continue to take his advice. The building was repaired in 2003 at a cost of ₹ 80,000; half of the contribution came from the Panchayat and other half from the Rural Employment Programme in 2003. A few rooms were added to the upper storey of the dispensary. During the year 2003–2004, a total of 13,142 patients took medical advice/help from the dispensary. The budget for medicines varies according to the number of patients; during the year 2003–2004, cost of medicines came to ₹ 8,500. The physician enjoys good rapport with the villagers and has access to the lady patients among the Rajput. Programmes in public health include organisation of Pulse Polio campaign, and the physician brought six other villages under this programme.

A sub-centre for allopathic treatment was also started in the village during the period Sangram Singh was the Sarpanch, and the health worker who was employed during that period continued to work for over 12 years. The sub-centre acquired its own building in 2001. In March 2004, those who made use of the facilities came to 242. In the area of family planning the sub-centre has been allotted ten cases per year for operations, and this target is met regularly. The sub-centre provides for different types of inoculation of infants, and school children, besides distribution of tablets to expectant mothers. In these matters, co-ordination with the Anganwadi is maintained. The health worker (ANM) lives in the building, and her services are available round the clock.

Health facilities are available in the nearby town Fateh Nagar and cases requiring healthcare beyond the first aid are taken to the town which has facilities also for maternity and childcare. A retired school teacher now has a son working in Fateh Nagar and his vehicle (motorcycle) in used for several purposes, including for visiting the town to provide healthcare.

The village by now makes use of both Ayurvedic and allopathic systems of medicine. It is a part of the public health system of the state and is a centre to which other villages are also linked for primary healthcare purposes. For needs beyond this stage, villagers make use of facilities in the nearby town and when needed travel even beyond.

In the district as a whole the number of allopathic centres was 447 in 1999–2000 and only 133 for Ayurvedic and Unani (Zila Sankhyikiya Roop Rekha 2001, p. 3); in the village under the study, the letter had an early start and the former came in a little later.

A Dairy Cooperative

A dairy cooperative was established in 1994. A list of owners of cattle was prepared for the Gram Panchayat, data for 128 families were collected and 74 were considered eligible for membership of the dairy. Its main activity was to collect milk from these families and later carry the milk to the district headquarter, Chittorgarh. The quantity of milk collected daily varies between 1 and 1.5 quintals. Payment is made weekly. The society provides the following facilities:

Improved cattle feed, inoculation and insurance cover for the cattle at the rate of ₹ 50 per year has been arranged for a cover of ₹ 5000. In case of death, the amount covered is ₹ 25,000. One of the informants got his cow insured for ₹ 50,000 and after its death he was able to raise a claim and get the policy amount of ₹ 50,000 reimbursed to him. Medical examination of the cattle takes place regularly; efforts have been made to bring in the *Murrah* buffalo from Haryana for improving the local cattle breed. The cooperative has a president, a vice-president and a secretary; there are three supervisors, one of them had professional training. There are seven other members of the organising committee, all of them from among the *Rajput* except one *Gadri*. The cooperative society provides scholarship to students of class 11 for ₹ 200. Bank's formality requires a guarantee before a loan is granted

The group as such is aware of the purpose of the loan, and exercises sufficient pressure on the creditor to pay back the instalments on the due date. Such a compliance in a small group reminds one of Durkheim's definition of social facts being external and coercive. Here externality is combined with what may be called internationalisation of group values when members meet and this is particularly true of women SHGs. The meeting acquires an additional character of intercommunication among themselves on all matters, trivial or significant, thereby acting as a clearing house for each other's information, anxieties and experiences of pain or pleasure.

Swayam Sahayata Samiti

Self-help groups in the villages came into being in the twenty-first century. The Rajput family took initiative and establishes Mateshwari Self-Help Group. It has 20 members, of whom two are women and one Jat, the rest being Rajput males. Each member contributes ₹ 500 to the general fund, and loans are advanced to the members as per their needs; a committee of five members assesses loan requests. Preference is given to cases connected with illness, death or marriage. The contribution of ₹ 500 per month is required to be deposited with the secretary by 7 pm of 10th day of the month. Timely payment is insisted upon; a penalty of ₹ 10 is levied for late payment by 5 minutes and ₹ 25 thereafter. The rate of interest is prescribed to be 1 per cent and has to be paid every month. The loan is expected to be repaid in 15 instalments. Devendra Pal Singh, an active young man, works as secretary of the group. As many as five persons had taken the loan by July 2000.

The first effort in establishing self-help groups was made with the establishment of a Parivar Bank in 2001. A contribution of ₹ 100 per month was decided upon, and defaulters would be required to pay 2 per cent interest after the 15th of every month. The loan has to be returned in 10 monthly instalments beginning with the next month. Thirteen persons took the membership of bank, all belonging to the Rajput family; ₹ 1300 was collected in the first instance. Males only took the membership.

Development of SHGs through the *Aanganvadi* centres was promoted especially to benefit the women of the village. Two such groups were set up in 2001 and three more in the year 2003. All the names symbolically include the Goddess of Wealth, Laxmi, in their nomenclature. The first one was called Raj Laxmi.

Here again, the initiative came from the Ranawat households, and all the 11 members came from this group. With each contributing ₹ 50, the total sum collected was ₹ 550, and it was then decided to open an account with Bank of Baroda in the neighbouring village. The second such group was also established on 10 December 2001 under the name 'Bhagya Laxmi Swayam Sahayata Samuh'. This has a *Ranawat* lady as chairperson with 12 other members drawn from five different caste groups, of whom six are Vaishnav who were earlier called the *Sadhu*, two *Suthar*, two *Khateek*, one *Rawat* and one *Kharol*. A *Vaishnav* lady is the treasurer whereas a *Suthar* member acts as a secretary; the total contribution was ₹ 650, with 13 members contributing ₹ 50 each. The two societies taken together indicate how the group of Ranawat families sets the pace for innovation and guides further diffusion. Of the other groups that joined the Vaishnavs are important as they have some urban connections and their coverage is almost total. The two *Suthar* families are basically carpenters and also have urban connection. The two *Khateek* families carry on some work in urban areas.

Thus, families with a house in the village and have urban connections provide the social base for the start of this programme in the village.

The year 2003 saw the rise of three more SHGs. The first group was Vijay Laxmi Swayam Sahayta Samiti; it has 13 members drawn from among the Rajput (6), *Vaishnav* (3), and one each from the *Kharol* and the *Jat*. The organisational part is controlled by two Vaishnav members acting as president and treasurer and a Jat member working as secretary. All the members contributed ₹ 100; accordingly, a sum of ₹ 1300 was collected. The group was setup on 10 October 2003. The next group is called Vaibhav Laxmi SSS; this was set up on 5 November 2003. It has 14 members drawn from among the Rajput, OBC, SC and ST. The initial contribution was ₹ 10 per member and the 14 members pooled together to come up with ₹ 140. A slightly more well-to-do group made a contribution of ₹ 20 each, and the members in this case were spread over the four groups mentioned above; this cooperative was set up on 5 December 2003. It was named Dhan Laxmi SSS and has a membership of 13 persons. The setting up of the last two groups indicate the growing reach of SHGs among the medium and lower-income groups in the village who made nominal contributions. By the end of 2003, coverage of the membership of SHGs through *Aanganvadi* had reached a total 64 women members in the village.

The general rules for an opening SHG require that they would meet every month on a fixed date and time, which is 10th of every month at 11 am at the *Aanganvadi* centre. The late-comers are to be fined ₹ 5 each; loans are to be repaid within 10 months with interest at the rate of 1 per cent. Loans will not be granted for child marriages or dinners after the death of a person. In this sense, the SHG can be treated as contributing to social reforms. The members can take the loan only for a reasonable purpose like treatment for illness and other necessities.

The SHG does not act with the formality of a regular bank where guarantee is required before a loan is granted. The group as such is aware of the purpose of the loan and exercises sufficient pressure on the creditor to pay back the instalments on due date. Such compliance in a small group reminds one of Durkheim's definition of social facts being external and coercive. Here externality is combined with what may be called internalisation of group values. When members meet, and this is particularly true of women SHGs, the meeting acquires an additional character of intercommunication among themselves on all matters, trivial or significant, thereby acting as a clearing house for each other's information, anxieties and experiences of pain or pleasure.

The experiment in developing SHGs marks the entry of the villagers in pooling together their resources for their own benefit. The involvement of such groups in small number of known persons enhances chances of greater cooperation and control. The association of the five SHGs with *Aanganvadi* centres adds to the process of the SHGs acquiring the characteristics of a formal institution and in turn the strengthening of the movement.

This SHG is an important addition to the village complex as it institutionalises secondary sources of income, not generally reported by the respondents. It adds a new dimension to the maintenance of ecological balance between man-land and plants-animals ratio.

The Village Panchayat and the Wider Policy

Ranawaton-ki-Sadri has been a part of the group of the five villages lumped together for the creation and operation of the Gram Panchayat under the Panchayati Raj institutional set-up.

The first demarcation included Nilod, Ranawaton-ki-Sadri, Jawa, and Anjan Kheda, with headquarters at Nilod. The second reorganisation brought together in 1955 a new set of five villages, namely, Patoliya, Ranawaton-ki-Sadri, Jawa, Anjan Kheda, and Bangla with headquarters at Patoliya. In the old revenue system, Patoliya belonged to the Khalsa category that was under the direct rule of the king. The names of the Sarpanch along with their caste and party affiliations and tenure are given in the following table.

Table 6.1

Caste and party affiliations of the Sarpanches of Gram Panchayats (for Sadri) 1977–2004

Name of Sarpanch	*Village*	*Seat of Panchàyat*	*Period*	*Caste*	*Party affiliation*
Sangram Singh	Sadri	Nilod	1977–1995	Rajput	Congress
Anand Kanwar	Sadri	Patoliya	1995–2000	Rajput	BJP
Bhairon Lal	Patoliya	Patoliya	2000–cont.	Maheshwari	BJP

Source: Info compiled during field work.

The *Gram Panchayat* elects a representative for the Panchayat Samiti at the block level. The nature of the constituency undergoes a change as some seats get reserved for special categories. This affects continuity in holding an office and a change in the nature of representation. A leading member with influence in neighbouring constituency may opt for it and try his or her chances. The details regarding membership of the *Panchayat Samiti* are summarised in the following table.

Table 6.2

*Members of the Panchayat Samiti Bhopal Sagar (for Sadri's neighbouring constituency) 1995–2000**

Name of Sarpanch	*Village*	*Seat of Panchayat*	*Period*	*Category*	*Caste*	*Party affiliation*
Sangram Singh	Sadri	Nilod	1995–2000	General	Rajput	Congress
Rameshwar	Nilod	Nilod	2000–cont.	SC		
Roop Singh	Sadri	Pari	2000–cont.	General	Rajput	BJP

Source: Information obtained through interviews with the village people.

It will be clear from the data presented in the two tables as to how the area of influence gets adjusted and continuity maintained in a multi-village organisation.

Developmental activities of the *Panchayat* are clearly visible in the changing contours of the village. The leadership gets credit for initiating social processes needed to mobilise human and financial resources. We may briefly allude to this aspect while summarising the four phases of development in the village with the changing leadership of the *Gram Panchayat*.

Phase I

1978–1979

Two *pakka* rooms were built for the village primary school. The village got electricity. Resources were arranged under Food-for-Work programme. The MLA of this constituency, Shyama Kumari Sengar, played a leading role in bringing electricity to the village.

1981

Drinking water facility for the twin villages of Kakarwa and Ranawaton-ki-Sadri was planned by the Sarpanch on the advice of S.S. Ranawat of Kakarwa, IAS, who happened to be in charge of the concerned department at the state level. Pipes were laid out and tube wells activated by 1985.

1983

An Ayurvedic dispensary was opened. Initially, the village Sarpanch provided housing facilities. The local MLA also supported this initiative.

A *kachha* approach road was built and the state of the streets was improved.

1984

A primary health sub-centre was opened. Congress MP, Nirmala Kumari Shaktawat, and the MLA, Shanker, played a leading role in this regard.

1986–1987

The region faced a famine during this period. With government funds, relief work was organised with the engagement of 450 labourers on daily wages. The Panchayat Samiti played a crucial role in combating this calamity.

1987–1990

Work in the adjacent villages which fell within the *Gram Panchayat* area was carried out. During this period, anicuts were constructed and electricity was provided to the SC and ST dwellings in the villages of Anjan Kheda, Nilod, Joheda, and the Dhola Data portion of Sadri.

Approach roads and bus stands were also constructed in all the villages forming part of the *Gram Panchayat*. Sadri has one bus stop across the railway track on the Fateh Nagar–Bhopal Sagar highway, which is named after Maharana Pratap. A signboard at the bus stop acknowledges the support given by the *Gram Panchayat* of Patoliya.

During this period, a primary school was also started in village of Anjan Kheda.

During phase I Sangram Singh happened to be the Sarpanch. The MLA also belonged to the Rajput group. An administrator in Jaipur was a kinsman from the same lineage at Kakarwa. This combination worked well. Sadri got electrified, got an approach road, a girls upper primary school, water supply, telephone connections, and the Ayurvedic health facility.

With a change in government at the state level, power equations changed. Nirmala Kumari Shaktawat, a lecturer in Sociology in Government Degree College, Chittorgarh, left her job and successfully contested for Lok Sabha. She belonged to the Rajput caste and found a partial entry in the political space in the village as well. The Sarpanch continued developmental works and formally joined the BJP and organised local support for it. The programmes initiated in the neighbouring villages stood him in good stead, as he got an entry through election from the group of five villages to the Panchayat Samiti for the period 1995–2000. He got support for developmental activities in the village, but his long-term of 18 years created an anti-incumbency factor. He could not make a good impression among the kinsmen who belonged to other political parties. The elections of 2000 saw the two groups in different camps, and an alliance with the neighbouring village of Patoliya to alternate the position of the Sarpanch among the two major villages tilted the balance.

Phase II

The first phase got an abrupt ending with the administration taking over the working of the Village Panchayat in 1993. However, developmental works continued. The village streets were paved, and a gravel approach road was constructed. The second phase thus provided a sort of a breather for political contests.

Phase III

The Panchayati Raj institutions in the state received further support from the state. As a consequence, Gram Panchayats were reorganised, with adequate provision for the inclusion of SC and ST members and increasing participation of women. Patoliya Gram Panchayat made provision for a woman to be the Sarpanch. An elderly lady by the name of Anand Kunwar, belonging to the Thakur lineage, was chosen as the Sarpanch. She had the active support of Advocate Roop Singh, who became the planner and executor of various developmental activities in the village.

During her tenure, the village streets were paved and cemented electric poles replaced the temporary poles of wood. The girls school was upgraded to the upper primary school level and became co-educational, and later, to middle school, providing education up to class 8.

Phase IV

The fourth phase began in the year 2000 during which time fresh elections to the Gram Panchayat were held.

The elected Sarpanch was formerly a school teacher. He belongs to the Maheshwari caste, which is primarily a trader group. Although this caste is in a minority in the village, the Sarpanch had a good reputation and people voted for him. The two positions of the *Up-Sarpanch* (deputy Sarpanch) went to the residents of Sadri.

On the developmental side, the school received the priority attention. The Panchayat spent money to improve the class rooms and verandas and to build a prayer hall.

The year 2001 saw a transformation of the village road into a paved coal-tar (*dammar*) road built under the Prime Minister's connecting-road scheme for a distance of 1.20 kilometres. The opening of the road was an event at which the Zila Parishad Chief and the MP were present. The main court yard in front of the Rawla and the village street also got a cement concrete layout, yet the space in between and the connecting road remains muddy for a distance of hardly 50 meters.

With different political parties being in power, and the village leadership changing hands, the Panchayati Raj institutions have continued to deliver goods that are visible to all. Internal competition has not come at the cost of development. Intimate knowledge about each other is a part of the game. Use of common facilities, and cooperation for collective efforts, become a part of habit. The village takes credit for being a developing unit in contrast to other neighbouring villages where competitors for power are well known. Factional politics in the villages of the neighbourhood marred developmental activities in them. In operating the Panchayati Raj System, various elements of the village social structure – lineages, other caste configuration, and factional alliances – play their roles. Villagers have begun taking part in state-and national-level elections. In the process, many village leaders have succeeded in having contacts with leaders of various parties. Such contacts are also used to get help for the welfare of the village community.

7

Negotiating with Increasing Complexities

The village with a sustaining base of social life has been modifying its own institutions and acquiring new ones using its internal strength to define its position in the networks with an increased density over its rural and urban surroundings.

Changes in the Population Profile

We have tried to briefly record the manner in which the doubling of the population over five decades (1955–2004) has caused (i) extension of the space for habitation (the families, compounds and neighbourhoods), and (ii) modification in social relations.

The change in the population composition has been quite significant. A few families have migrated, and others have come in. This has also affected the caste composition of the village. This village, like several others in the region, has been a home to the Bhil tribals suggesting that the interactions of the tribal groups with the people living in the villages and the towns is not a new phenomenon in this region. In fact, the Bhils residing in the village are also treated as one of the castes; their interactions with other castes leads one to believe that the imagined isolation of the tribals from the other castes was broken long ago. Migrations of families of different castes – their arrivals and departures – have been at the individual initiative of the persons concerned. The various families of the village participate in some sort of give-and-take relationship, and it is not new and only the pace has increased. People leave the village in search of new urban jobs, and others come to the village to settle and work in their area of specialisation. The rise of new institutions in the village, as well as in the neighbouring villages and towns, has further enhanced the process. The Panchayati Raj institutions have made it structurally necessary for the village to meaningfully negotiate with groups of villages, the block headquarters, or the Tehsils, the district, and the state capital. The political process at the State Assembly and Parliamentary levels and the extension of work by the recognised national parties to rural areas have generated connecting links with the village, influencing the developmental activities at the village level. Incorporation of these new elements into the rural structure needs corresponding response on the part of students of rural India. This calls for a fresh perspective and use of additional sources of information.

A restudy requires use of secondary data generated during the interregnum and comparing it with the previous data. Such an exercise provides meaningful hints regarding structural-processual continuities.

The Physical Extensions of the Habitat

A revisit to the village after a lapse of nearly 50 years gives the feeling that too much has changed. The population of the village has been steadily increasing over the last five decades and has almost doubled. As many as 34 houses now form a new colony towards the south of the village and is named *Dhola-Danta* signifying the physical characteristics of the area where white stones with sharp edges abound. The *Basti* is referred to as Rampura, which has now a new look with several *pakka* houses. In this renovated old habitat, one notices a synthetic water tank built by the village *Panchayat*. There is now a *kachha* road in the southern part that links the village with Patoliya – the seat of the *Gram Panchayat*. A few more extensions occurred in the southern direction of the area now referred to as *Kala Bhata* because the area is abound by black stones. On the northern side, along the link road, the Rajput families have built *pakka* houses that give a new look to the village. This area was once used as a common place for thrashing grains. On the other side, an impressive school building has come up. This has, in fact, become the entry point for the village. The new habitation is called *Khala Chaperda* – this was earlier the common thrashing area (*Khala* – खल – refers to barn).

The main habitation has now several *pakka* houses with modern look and nice sanitary fittings, indicators of urbanisation. The qualitative improvements and extensions have been the consequence of increased urban contacts of the villagers. Those who have gone out to work but still maintain connections with their parental homes have been the carriers of modernity in the village. With increasing visits to nearby towns the villagers have become agents of urbanisation and of change.

There is an important section in the village population that commutes to work every day. This includes teachers and lawyers, a few contractors, and a fair section of the young literates who do jobs in towns.

The presence of retired persons adds to the pool of persons of proven merit to the human resources in the village.

In addition, 15 widows receive pensions from pay centres located outside the village. Such an exposure to the banking process has also remarkably affected their orientation. This group has played a leading role in organising women's self-help groups. Some women residents have become teachers and are posted in nearby larger villages where they commute daily.

Such trends in the village indicate the widening and diversification of avenues of resource organisation and cognition of the wider world.

Rural-Rural Interactions

In the changing milieu, interactions take place between the residents of the neighbouring villages as well as with the urban centres in the vicinage. A researcher has, therefore, the responsibility to study both rural-rural and rural-urban interactions, modifying the earlier format of rural-urban continuum. In the process of the hamlet acquiring the characteristics of the community, outside groups join the locals in making full use of the available natural and human resources.

As we mentioned, the Ranawat family had moved from the parental seat of power in Sanwad to this village, a number of artisans and service groups from the parental village continued their relationship with their clients in the new setting. Initially, these families stayed back in the old village but paid frequent visits to serve their masters in the new village. Later, most of them also moved to the new settlement. Of course, the Village Chief monitored this process. The businessmen, liquor vendors and domestic assistants from the Daroga families were generally discouraged to settle in the new village. They, however, encouraged the carpenter, blacksmith and potters to settle in the new habitat. A major section of the Jat from the neighbouring village of *Patoliya* shifted to the village pursuing their traditional vocation of agriculture. The *Sadhu* families moved in as caretakers of the village temple. However, the priestly functions of the Purohit were performed by a *Brahmin* family from the neighbouring village of Patoliya. The drummer, hailing from the *Dholi* caste, comes from *Aanjan Kheda*. The village practices exogamy as most of the families in different castes belong to a common patri-lineage. The only exceptions are the Bhils and the Jat who are larger in numbers and, who are represented by different lineages, making it possible to marry within the village but in different gotras within the caste. In other smaller caste groups gotra exogamy coincides with village exogamy.

The village also gets connected to other villages in times of disease, calamities, treatment of snakebite and mental disabilities. They still maintain the superstition that they are caused by the wrath of gods and goddesses and, therefore, they need to be appeased. However, people are not averse to medical treatment. Actions are taken on both the fronts: appeasement of deities and approved medical treatment – Ayurvedic or Allopathic. Since the shrines of deities known for the cure of specific ailments are located at different places, villagers take their patients to them and seek their blessings with the hope that such visits will assist in speedy recovery of the patient.

Within the region, *Matrikundia* has developed as a prominent pilgrim centre. People with limited means go there to immerse the ashes of the deceased. Almost all the castes of the region, belonging to different *varnas* (sects), have built their *Dharmshalas* (religious inns) there for the pilgrims. This pilgrim centre is visited by people from over a hundred villages of the region. The *Rajput* of the village have built through family-level contributions one such building at Narsinghdwara. On the walls are inscribed the names of persons who have donated ₹ 501 or more. The entries include half-a-dozen names from the village under study. These traditional networks are being extended in other directions as well. For example, the *Rajputs* have set up a Kshatriya Maha Sabha; one of the important leaders of the village understudy acts as the Secretary of its branch that covers a few villages, including the village under study.

Rural-rural interactions have acquired new dimensions in the organisational and institutional setup of the administration through Panchayat Raj institutions. The village *Panchayat* is formed for a group of settlers having a combined population of about 5,000. Village Ranawaton-ki-Sadri, along with four other villages, constitutes the village Panchayat with headquarters at Patoliya.

The constituency of the *Panchayat Samiti* is reserved for the Scheduled Castes (SCs). It is at present headed by a person from the village named Nilod. In order to remain powerful, the *Rajput* leadership joined the neighbouring constituency where they got elected. The elected members of the *Panchayat Samiti* widen their area of interactions to other nearby villages. Administratively, there is a *Patwari* (a village clerk who maintains village land records) who operates in his own circle of villages for revenue collections and to regulate the Public Distribution System (PDS), particularly for the weaker sections of the society.

The Police Department has its own setup, operating through the *Thanas* (police posts). The revenue administration through its Tehsil Headquarters connects various villages in two Panchayat Samiti areas and then there is the district headquarters where, besides administration, the Zila Parishad is also located.

The village has a middle school; its teachers hail from other villages or townships. The school organises Tehsil-level competitions in games and sports, playing host to 27 teams. The visits of such a large number of students and teachers from other places creates an atmosphere of a festival and promotes inter-village interactions. Such a function is also attended by the Chief of Zila Parishad, the MP, the MLA and other officials of the government.

Developmental works are carried out in the village through the *Panchayat Samiti*, individual contributions and state assistance. The public distribution system works through a contractor who supplies food grains at subsidised rates to the families of a group of villages covered by the *Patwari*. Village leadership assists in the process and thus enhance their visibility and promote their influence. A retired headmaster of a government school, who now lives in his parental village, voluntarily supervises the distribution at the village level.

The local leadership had taken steps to (a) upgrade the school, (b) set up primary schools in other small villages and (c) promote construction of link roads to enhance the connectivity of the villages. Elections to the office of the Chairperson, or *Pradhan* of the *Panchayat*

Samiti, also promote people's participation. The elected leaders exercise their influence in getting grants for developmental works.

The village leadership maintains connections with the MLAs and the MPs of the region as well as with the elected representatives of the Zila Parishad to ensure state support for the development of their constituency. In the past, these connections have helped in improving the water supply scheme, getting electricity and phone connections in the village, upgrading of the village school, and in the renovation of the school building with clean space for drinking water and better sanitary facilities, particularly for the girls. The village now wears a new look. It is important to mention that the change of political leadership has not adversely affected the village development process. This is not so in the neighbouring large villages where the streets have dirty roads, market is small and banking facilities are limited. Larger villages are characterised by political factionalism that hampers the development process. It is in this sense that the ushering in of the Panchayati Raj institutions has further facilitated the process of rural development.

The rise of the new buildings in the village has provided opportunities for jobs to a new set of workers. Even it has facilitated adoption of new skills replacing the caste-associated low-grade traditional jobs. In particular, people of the so-called lower castes doing menial and filthy jobs have found new avenues for work in the construction sector. Skilled workers in the field of construction are available in large neighbouring villages and townships. Similarly, the young of this village go to other villages and towns for work in the modern sector of the economy. They run auto rickshaws, work at construction sites in various roles – from daily wage to skilled jobs as carpenters, electricians, *Mistries* and plumbers. Special mention may be made of school teachers from the village going to work in other villages as well as a few from other villages coming to work in the village under study. The use of modern vehicles has facilitated travel to long distances. With opportunities available for Girls' education beyond class 8 in two neighbouring villages, some girl students have gone for higher education.

Health centres organise a number of special programmes such as smallpox and polio vaccine. The village dispensary provides both Ayurvedic and allopathic medicines. In the initial stages a female worker from Kerala had come to the village and stayed there. At the time of our study, a person ran the Ayurvedic centre; he daily commuted from his place of residence to the village. The village has thus begun to interact with other villages in two ways: (1) sending out people for work to other villages, and (2) receiving villagers from the neighbouring settlements to work in the village. This two-way interaction is increasing with the developmental works in the region.

Rural-Urban Articulations

The villagers have been looking out for work in various prestigious occupations of the day. Thus, one of the village residents became a ranger in the Forest Department. His first son also followed suit; second one joined teaching. His brother joined the state service and became Naib Tehsildar. One of his nephews became an Ameen – a land revenue clerk. Another one joined as hostel superintendent in a school. Still another joined the Army and participated in the Second World War. Another member of this family joined the education department and retired as headmaster of the government secondary school; his relative retired as an inspector in the Department of Land Records.

Persons with lesser education opted for the jobs of a policemen and security guards. One became a driver in the railways and another a truck driver. Spread over three generations altogether 15 persons from this lineage have served outside the village. All these have unfortunately died.

The most notable among them was a person who was trained in dairy management in New Zealand and who served as a dairy manager in a company near New Delhi.

The trend towards modernisation is more explicit in the younger generations of these pioneers who have passed away. Besides the 15 deceased persons, 57 others have taken jobs outside the village; among them there are two women who work as teachers. Another woman is in-charge of the village *Anganwadi*. Two persons who have completed their MA and BA degrees, respectively, have joined the tourist trade; one of them has developed efficiency in speaking French, which is useful in his dealings with clientele coming from the French-speaking countries.

This brief history of a Rajput lineage demonstrates the advantage of an early start. According to their education and training, people of this lineage joined various jobs and got exposed to the waves of modernisation and though them the village also got vicariously introduced to the new trends.

Exposure to the wider world is confined not only to the *Rajput* families; the trend is spreading among other castes as well. There are 10 persons belonging to the Jat caste who work as helpers in shops and canteens elsewhere: six of them work in Mumbai, three in the nearby town of Fateh Nagar and one in Ahmedabad.

The *Vaishnav* group has sent out two persons: one to Kuwait and another to Muscat. Another person has joined a voluntary organisation. Their educational levels range from class 7 to class 10.

Ten *Gadri* boys are at present working at other places, generally as shop assistants; they have completed 7–8 years of schooling. Similarly, among the *Suthar* group, two have gone out to work as carpenters in Fateh Nagar and Muscat, respectively, which their caste-bound traditional work. They have also studied up to middle school. Among the *Teli*, a boy works as an assistant in a jewellery shop in the neighbouring town. Similarly, a *Keer* boy left his studies after completing class 8 and is doing the traditional caste-bound job of growing vegetables and fruits in Saudi Arabia.

The *Khateeks* of the village have done well. Ten young men of this caste have gone to Gujarat: two to Ahmedabad, and rest to Baroda. They have their own trolleys to do peripatetic vending. They have done some schooling. Two persons from the *Balmiki* caste work as peons in Udaipur.

The total number of workers outside the village by caste is as follows: *Rajput* 72 (of whom 15 are deceased), 10 each from among the Jat and the *Gadri*, 9 *Khateek*, 3 *Vaishnav*, 2 each from among the *Suthar* and the *Balmiki*, and 1 each from among the *Teli* and *Keer* castes.

It is the people from the *Rajput* caste who have been exposed to the urban life for a longer period extending to four generations. Among the *Rajputs*, two levels of economic standard are visible almost corresponding to their educational standards.

Among other castes, there is nobody who has studied in a college. Those who are somewhat educated have gone to urban centres seeking jobs according to their training. Some have found new avenues to practise their caste-bound occupation in a strange setting either within India or in abroad. It is only the *Rajputs* who have people with college education and who have opted for government jobs in the service sector.

The overall position of the presence of nearly a hundred persons in the village with urban placements, and maintaining relations with the village, mark the new way of life in the village. The acquisition of urban facilities for their rural households has substantially influenced the village site. The improvements in transport and communications have brought the village closer to the urban centres.

Several households in the village now possess vehicles of different sorts, including motorcycle, scooter, car, jeep and tempo. The residents have also acquired tractors, thrashers and boring machines to modernise agriculture. A total of 85 such units are available in the village and are mostly (52 units) owned by the Rajputs. Others are owned by families belonging to the Jat (6 units), *Gadri* (4 units), 3 each by the *Vaishnav Sadhus* and the *Kalal*, and 2 each by the *Teli*, *Suthar* and the *Bhil*. One family runs the flower mill; another uses the sewing machine for stitching clothes of the village clients. The oil-presser caste of Teli have replaced the traditional oil-presser by an oil-extracting machine and a thrasher which is rented out.

It is important to mention that the village has families with their own mechanised transport for travel or carrying load. The bullock cart is thus gradually being replaced by cycles, mopeds and scooters.

A special mention must be made of the families of the Khatik who own 10 vehicles for visiting places for work or for other social gatherings in the neighbourhood. This group is more advanced in terms of acquiring the motorised vehicles proportionately to its size in the village population.

Among the Rajput households, there are 52 power-driven vehicles and machines. Thirteen of the families have more than one vehicle. One family owns three cars, two of which are used as taxies in the town of Udaipur and another is kept for family use. Most of the vehicles are used for commuting to their work places. Three tractors are used for cultivation in own lands and another three are given on rent to other farmers. Two families have boring machines which are given on rent. There is a crane and a water tanker in the village which are rented out. The availability of the modern means of transport has facilitated inter-village interactions and helped in enlarging their cognitive horizons.

New Elements in the Social Structure

In the developmental process, there is a need to acknowledge the pivotal role played by the state. The state has aided in capacity building and in the mobilisation of human resources. In recent years, the development activities initiated in the village have prompted various officials and political leaders to pay frequent visits to the village. These visits have opened a new channel of communication between the villagers and the bureaucracy. These connections have enabled the local elite to participate in the wider polity and to use these connections for the good of the village community. The approach road to the village, availability of water supply and electricity, and connectivity via telephone and mobile phones have broken the relative isolation of village communities. The village now has many new institutions such as village middle school, an Anganvadi and a primary health sub-centre along with an Ayurvedic dispensary. The institutions of the Panchayati Raj have helped the village develop a democratic political culture. Between the 1950s – when the village was first studied – and the beginning decade of the twenty-first century the face of the village has so much changed that the previous description appears dated.

In the first phase of ushering in the democratic polity, elections to the state legislature and the parliament were like a routine, and the election process was beyond their comprehension. This was more so in the case of women who hesitated to go to the polling booth to cast their vote. For the enlightened males, the elections were significant for their vote but they could hardly think of contesting for a seat. The small beginning made by the introduction of Panchayati Raj, as part of the democratic decentralisation, initially attracted the traditional chiefs but not the common people. It took more than two decades for the process of decentralisation of power and its links with rural development programmes to become sufficiently attractive for common people. However, local elite grabbed the new positions. Later, provision of reservations for women and for the SCs enlisted participation of many who were hitherto denied such a privilege. Thereafter, competitive processes began working. To promote inter-caste collaboration the leaders of various factions made efforts to enlist the support of villagers. As the constituency of the *Gram Panchayat* covers five villages, inter-village connections became important with understanding being reached for successive sharing of power. A local elite sought a neighbouring consistency of five villages for representation in the wider *Panchayat Samiti* at the block level. The phase of intense competition among the local elite has set in and connections with the state-level political parties have been established. Such new forces have given a different look to the social morphology of the village. However, all the factional leaders agree that the developmental process has strengthened in the village. The village has shown visible improvements in the quality of public services and institutions. The emergence of the new elements and their incorporation into the village life has created new avenues of cooperation with other villages and towns and instigated the local elites to play an active role in managing human and material resources for the betterment of village community. The village no longer looks like a *Jagir*, although it has its vestiges. The village is in the process of transition.

What has been happening to the traditional institution of caste? The basic attribute of caste as an endogamous entity has not been affected in the rural milieu, while inter-caste marriages are becoming more common in the cities. Villages being smaller in size have families of different castes, but these families generally belong to a common exogamous lineage necessitating marriage in other villages but within their own caste. This pattern has not changed.

Socially speaking, castes in the non-twice-born Varnas permit widow marriages/remarriages, and the custom of making gifts of ornaments to the bride is retained. At the time of remarriage of a widow, this becomes a major point of contention which is resolved through the intervention of the caste Panchayat. Since the prices of precious metal – gold and silver – have escalated several times, the value of ornaments has also increased. The settlement of disputes related to the amount to be given to the re-marrying bride now takes two to three years. People have also begun taking recourse to the civil court. In terms of inter-village relations castes have shown vitality in strengthening their units of cooperation, like the *Chokhala* or the new ones like their Caste Sabha. In the village setting, people still ask for one's caste to figure out the manner of interaction with a visitor. But in a township, particularly in big cities a person's caste has ceased to be a key consideration in interactions.

A Synoptic View

We return to the question that took us back to the village that was studied more than 50 years ago. What has happened to the village during the interregnum? How does the village look like in the first decade of the twenty-first century? And in what manner do approaches to the study of the village get modified in the process.

It is self-evident that the generation of the school-going children of the 1950s are now nearing the end of their journey and playing different roles related to old age – retirement, staying back home to spend time with grandchildren, leading a restful life or battling with ailments associated with old age. Structural units like family, lineage and caste continue to exist, though their functioning has been affected by waves of change and modern values. We were reminded of the necessity of using the historical approach for understanding the elements of social structure. It was particularly relevant in the case of *Rajput* families who had to move from a feudal culture to the democratic way of living.

We have historically traced the lineage of the founders of this village from the time the lineage branched off from the princely family of the ruler of Mewar some seven generations ago. The resulting knowledge about the vertical dimensions of the lineage and the multiplication of families of the lineage settling in other villages helped us understand the continuity of exogamous relations and solidarity at the lineage level. Events connected with marriage and death provide an occasion for the members of the vast lineage to meet and renew their relationships. It is important that though this group shows unity at times of family functions, the lineage members belong to different political parties. For gathering support in the political sphere, they seek support of people from other castes. Such a situation defies popular notion that castes vote en bloc to a given dispensation. Vote bank politics may be a strategic tool for the contenders, but it is not necessary that the voters oblige such overtures.

The doubling of population and its effort at finding space within the settlement has, in fact, widened the habitation area. The family units gets reorganised and continue their membership in the old compound and rights in the parental land, but they also look out for additional economic opportunities and education for their children, supplementing their earnings to finance the modern/urban component in the houses. This has also affected their lifestyle.

The units of social structure entail both organising forces and creating avenues for expression of dissent and competitive actions. Over the years, many changes have been made by individual families in the celebration of events and conduct of family functions. Many out-migrant families observe these rituals and celebrate family functions at the place of their migration rather than returning to the village. This is not viewed favourably by the families still living in the village. With official taboo on the organisation of death feasts, those living elsewhere carry out eschatological rituals at the place of their stay rather than coming to the village so far away from where they live currently. At best, family members may come to visit the shrines of family deities.

Some other points of significance may be briefly mentioned:

1. There is now scope for carrying out conflict studies. It may be an extension of the approach to study factions. Study of factions was first carried out in village studies by Oscar Lewis (1958) and Yogesh Atal (1968).
2. Information regarding death is now being sent through mail. While in the cities, the photograph of the dead is also printed, the villagers rejected this innovation on the ground that the letter may be destroyed and thus the picture of the dead may be dishonoured. Now news of the death are relayed on the local television in Udaipur, and this medium is also being used by some eminent villagers.

3. Death feasts in the village are also halted after the state ruling. However, people have found alternate ways of substituting this practice. Rich families organise it as a feast to welcome the pilgrims returning after a bath in the river Ganga.

The Relevance of the Study: Theoretical and Methodological Gains and Implications for Policymaking

It is our view that longitudinal studies provide a better understanding of the social reality compared to the one-shot studies. While the policymakers are always in a hurry to plan and implement their programmes utilising whatever is available, we believe that the study of villages in depth over a period of time provides a different 'baseline'. This is supported by some senior bureaucrats. For example, speaking in a 2003 Seminar organised by our team, Jagat Mehta, former Foreign Secretary, admitted that when policies were drawn for rural development in the early years of India's independence, policymakers were handicapped by the paucity of basic literature for certain regions. We were not aware of the region-specific requirements and focussed on all-India plans. He stressed on the need for basic in-depth studies to provide analytical insights.

Policies ought to be distinguished from 'programmes' based on them. Authentic studies are needed to formulate policies. We believe that such studies need to be continuously supported by national bodies like the ICSSR and centres of higher learning in their own programmes.

The specific directions in which the present study calls for greater attention of the policymakers are the following:

1. Programmes of action get related to a complex set of local variations and local history. There is need to develop area-specific plans and programmes.
2. A part of the programme monitoring needs in-depth case studies.
3. With increasing insistence on a sociologist being associated with the planning and execution of large-scale multinational projects, it is imperative that sociologists on their own continue to conduct in-depth studies. As multinationals are bigger users of data to take decisions, they would welcome rigorous and in-depth studies in each region.
4. The relationship between serious research efforts and the planners and policymakers needs to be established as an on-going process. State-level workshops needs to be organised to discuss social science field researches with a view to identifying their policy relevance. Sociologists may take lead in this regard and convene interdisciplinary seminars with the participation of researchers from disciplines like economics, history, geography, public administration and political science. The required financial support should be provided by the ICSSR and other concerned bodies.
5. The ICSSR and the district/state administration need to promote area-specific programmes of research.
6. The Panchayati Raj institutions have to cope with situations where political parties of different orientations work at various tiers of polity.
7. The working of the Gram Panchayats is basically an inter-village activity. Therefore, studies of the

Panchayat must be carried out at the level of Panchayat area and not a single village.

8. On the specific side, there continues to be a need for conducting interdisciplinary training programmes in social science research methodology of a reasonable duration, say four to five weeks, with half the emphasis on conducting field studies/representing of data into meaningful presentations. In its earlier days, ICSSR did launch such a programme and held about 13 such programmes every year. The present practice of one-week training opted by the ICSSR is no substitute for the original programme.

The present study has been helpful in bringing together findings in history, economics and sociology. It is suggested that collaborative efforts be made in promoting 'area studies'. The experiment in having a 'planning forum' in the past be activated at multidisciplinary levels and innovations in the syllabus that look for 'practical' aspects be made part of the curriculum.

Theoretical and methodological gains of enquiry may be briefly recalled. First, the study combined historical and structural-functional approaches. It is a study of changing the configuration of structural units continuously causing a fresh balance. However, it is difficult to call the process as one of *structuration* because structures were already in existence; what is new and different is changing functions in the already-existing structures as well as admitting new structural elements to meet new needs.

The study employed traditional tools of inquiry like observation, case studies and genealogies. It carried out long informal interviews and collected census data from all the households of the village. The team also participated in many important events that took place during its stay in the village. The richness of the historical material, particularly available in former princely state, added to the possibility of going beyond 'conjectural history'. The sources acquired sociological relevance through their careful reinterpretation. The information about new activities promoted by the state as well as by the voluntary agencies was also very useful.

References

Atal, Y. (1968) *Changing Frontiers of Castes*. National Publishing House, New Delhi.

Bailey, F.G. (1995) *Caste and the Economic Frontier*. Oxford University Press, London.

Beteille, A. (1966) *Caste, Class and Power: Changing Patterns of Stratification in a Tanjore Village*. Oxford University Press, Bombay.

Chauhan, B.R. (1961) A Study of a Social Institution in an Indian Village. *Rural Sociology*, 26, 191–197.

Chauhan, B.R. (1961) Chokhala – An Inter-Village Organisation: A Caste in Rajasthan. *Sociological Bulletin* (13 September, No. 2).

Chauhan, B.R. (1967) *A Rajasthan Village*. Associated Press, Delhi.

Chauhan, B.R. (1988) *Bharat Main Gramin Samaj*. A.C. Brothers, Udaipur, Rajasthan, India.

Chauhan, B.R. (1990) *Rural Urban Articulations*. A.C. Brothers, Udaipur, Rajasthan, India.

Chauhan, B.R. (1999) *A Rajasthan Village* (2nd ed.). A.C. Brothers, Udaipur, Rajasthan, India.

Chauhan, B.R. (2001) *Muslims in Meerut Revisited: A Report Submitted to ICSSR, New Delhi*. Institute of Social Development, Udaipur, Rajasthan, India.

Court of Upper District Judge, II, Chittorgarh (2001) *Copy of the Orders of the Civil Suit P.S. 65/99 (CM 38)*, dated 12.10.2001.

Das, V. (1982) *Structure and Cognition: Aspects of Hindu Caste and Ritual*. Oxford University Press, New Delhi.

Desai, I.P. (1977) The Vedchi Movement. In I.P. Desai and Banwari Lal Chaudhry (eds), *History of Rural Development in Modern India* (Vol. 2). Impex India, New Delhi.

Dube, S.C. (1955) *Indian Village*. Routledge and Kegan Paul, London.

Dube, S.C. (1958) *India's Changing Villages: Human Factors in Community Development*. Routledge and Kegan Paul, London.

Dumont Louis. (2004) *Homo Hierarchicus: The Caste System and Its Implications*. Oxford University Press, New Delhi.

Election Commission. (2001) *Voters List, 2004 Ranawaton-Ki-Sadari, Assembly Constituency (2001)* Kapasan, Code 123, Part 66.

Epstein, S.T. (1978) *South India: Yesterday, Today and Tomorrow*. The English Language Book Society and Macmillan, New Delhi.

Epstein, S.T., Suryanarayana, A.P. and Thimmegowda, T.T. (1998) *Village Voices: Forty Years of Rural Transformation in South India*. Sage, New Delhi.

Government of Rajasthan. (2001) *Zila Sankhyiki Rooprekha 2001 District Chittorgarh*, Directorate of Economics and Statistics, Jaipur, Rajasthan, India.

Government Upper Primary School. (2003) *Monthly Enrolment of Boys and Girls*, October 2003, Ranawaton-ki-Sadari, District Chittorgarh, Rajasthan, India.

Gram Panchayat Ranawaton Ki Sadari. (1997–1998) *List of Persons below the Poverty Line* (Serial number 3269–3368).

Gupta, D. (ed.). (2004) *Social Stratification*. Oxford University Press, New Delhi.

Krishi Ganana. (2001–2002) *Rajasthan: Niwasi Jotdharakon Avam Unke Kshetraphal Ki Suchi*, Village Ranawaton Ki Sadari, Patvar Mandal Patolia, R.N. Mandal, Kakarwa, Tehsil Kapasan, District Chittorgarh, Rajasthan, India.

Leach, E.R. (1954) *Political System of High Land Burma*. Beacon, Boston, MA.

Lerner, D. (1964) *The Passing of Traditional Society*. Free Press, New York.

Lewis, O. (1958) *Village Life in Northern India*. University of Illinois Press, Urbana.

Madan, V. (2002) *The Village in India*. Oxford University Press, New Delhi.

Marriott M. (ed.). (1955) *Village India: Studies in Little Communities*. Chicago University Press, Chicago, IL.

Mathur, K.S. (1961) Meaning of Religion in a Malwa Village. In L.P. Vidyarathi (ed.), *Aspects of Religion in Indian Society*. EFCS, Lucknow, UP, India.

Oommen, T.K. (2002) *Pluralism, Equality and Identity: Comparative Studies*. Oxford University Press, New Delhi.

Ranawaton Ki Sadari Milk Producers Cooperative Federation Ltd. (n.d.) *Pashupalako Ka Varghikaran*, Kapasan.

Shyamaldas. (1888) *Veer Vinod*. Saraswati Pustakalay, Udaipur, Rajasthan, India.

Srinivas, M.N. (1952) *Religion and Society among Coorgs of South India*. Oxford University Press, New Delhi.

Srinivas, M.N. (1955) The Social System of Mysore Village. In M. Marriott (ed.), *Village India*. Chicago University Press, Chicago, CL.

Srinivas, M.N. (1976) *The Remembered Village*. Oxford University Press, New Delhi.

Srinivas, M.N. (2002) *Village, Caste, Gender and Method*, Oxford University Press, New Delhi.

Annexures

Annexure 1: Location of Rajasthan Village (Map of Study Area)

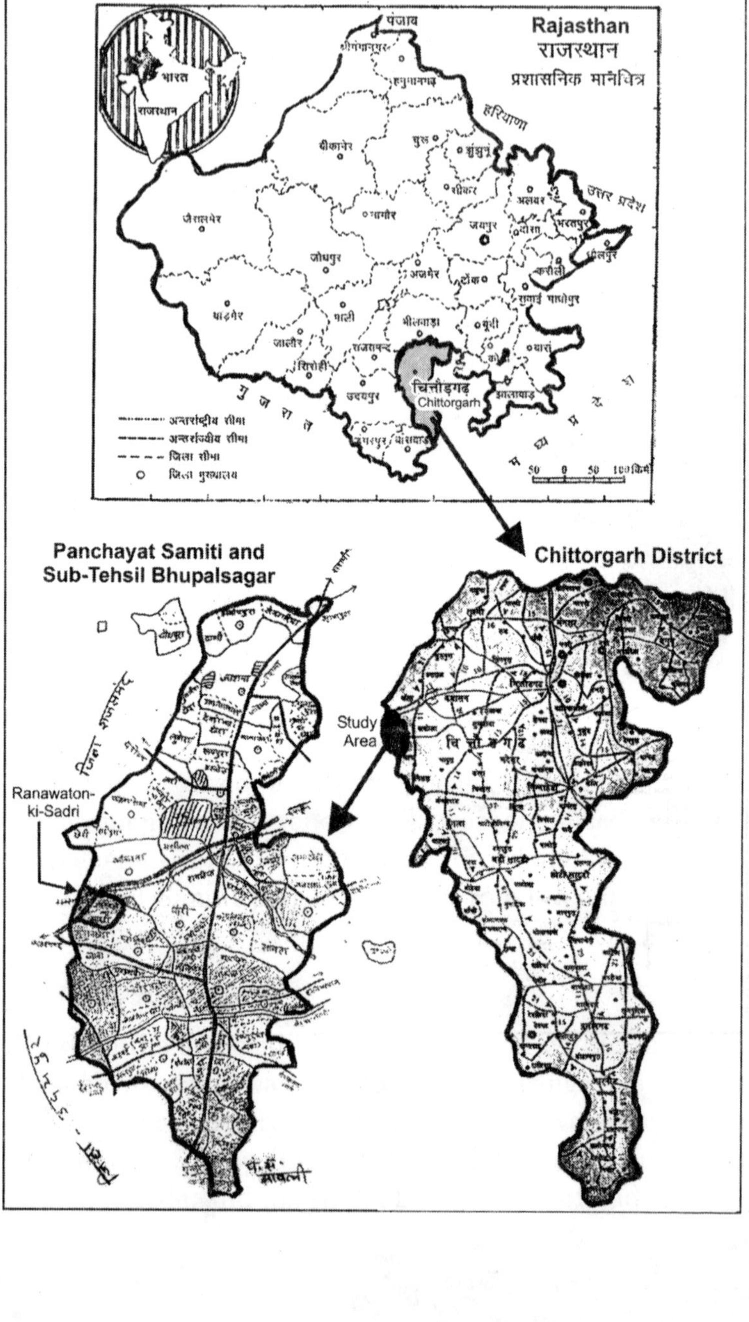

Annexure 2: Sketch Map of the Village Habitation

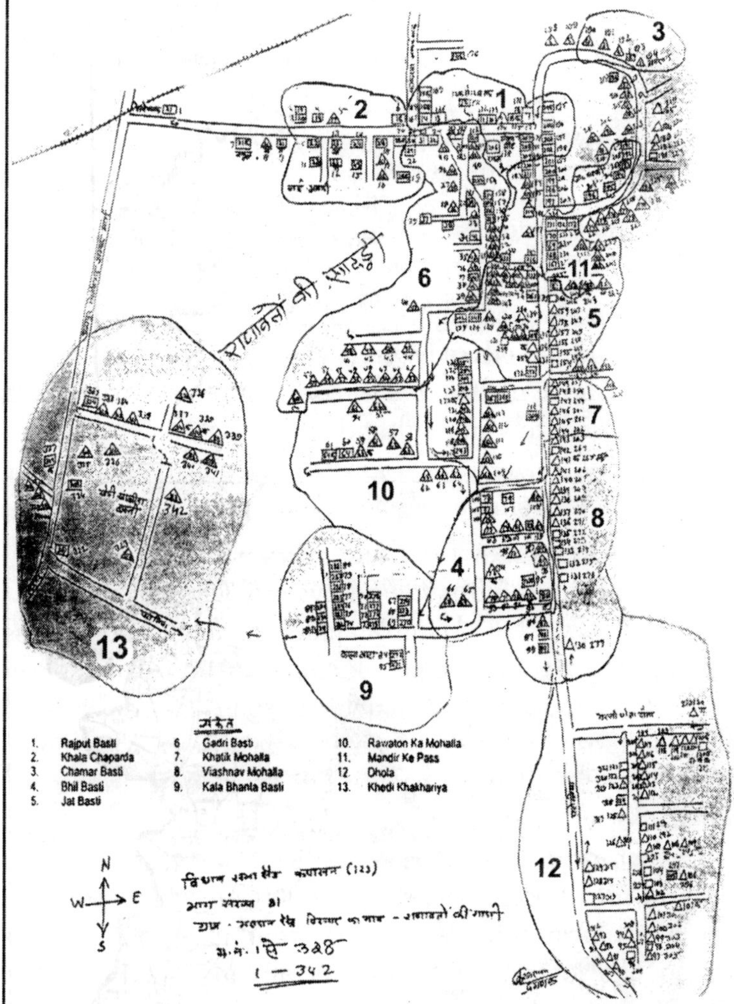

Annexure 3: Record of Offsprings of Maharana Udaisinghji

बाज़बहादुरके यहां रहनेसे बादशाही फ़ौजें आआकर उदयपुर पर हमला करने लगीं. विक्रमी १६२७ [हि० ९७८ = ई० १५७०] में महाराणा कुंभलमेर पधारे फिर वहांसे फ़ौज एकट्ठीकरके गोगूंदे आये और विक्रमी १६२८ का दशहरा वहीं किया. यह महाराणा जब फाल्गुन महीनेमें कुछ बीमार हुए तो इन्होंने अपने पुत्र जगमालको जो महाराणी भटियाणीसे जन्माथा युवराज बनाया, क्योंकि महाराणी भटियाणी पर इन महाराणाकी ज़ियादह मिहरबानी थी. विक्रमी १६२८ फाल्गुन शुक्ल १५ [हि० ९७९ ता० १४ शव्वाल = ई० १५७२ ता० २८ फ़ेब्रुअरी] को महाराणा उदयसिंहका देहान्त हुआ.

इन महाराणाके मिज़ाज (स्वभाव) में स्थिरता बहुत कम थी और ये अक्ल व बहादुरीमें अपने बाप महाराणा सांगासे चौथे हिस्से भी नहीं थे परन्तु विक्रमादित्यसे अच्छे थे इसलिये इनकी निन्दा नहीं हुई.

कर्नेल् टॉडसाहबके लिखनेके अनुसार बहुत कायर भी नहीं थे क्योंकि इन्होंने लड़ाइयोंमें अक्सर बहादुरीका काम किया. इन महाराणाका जन्म विक्रमी १५७९ भाद्रपद शुक्ल १० [हि० ९२८ ता० ९ शव्वाल = ई० १५२२ ता० ४ ऑगस्ट] को और विक्रमी १६२८ फाल्गुन शुक्ल १५ [हि० ९७९ ता० १४ शव्वाल = ई० १५७२ ता० २८ फ़ेब्रुअरी] को देहान्त हुआ.

इनके २४ महाराजकुमार थे, सोनगरा अक्षयराजकी बेटी जैवंताबाईके गर्भ से महाराजकुमार १ प्रतापसिंह, सज्जाबाई सोलंखिणीके २ शक्तिसिंह ३ वीरमदेव, जैवंताबाई मादड़ेचीका बेटा ४ जैतसिंह, करमचंद प्रमारकी बेटी लालाबाईका बेटा

महाराणा उदयसिंह.] वीरविनोद. [राज पीपलां—८७

५ कान्ह, वीरबाई झालीका बेटा ६ रायसिंह, लक्खाबाई झालीके बेटे ७ शार्दूलसिंह ८ रुद्रसिंह, धीरबाई भटियाणीके बेटे ९ जगमाल, १० सगर, ११ अगर, १२ साह, १३ पच्याण, इसीतरह १४ नारायणदास, १५ सुल्तान्, १६ लूणकरण, १७ महेशदास, १८ चंदा, १९ भावसिंह, २० नेतसिंह, २१ नगराज, २२ बैरीशाल २३ मानसिंह और २४ साहिबखां नामके थे– कुल राणियां १८ जिनसे कुल २४ बेटे वग़ैरह औलादथी (१).

(१) इन चौबीसोंमें से कई एकके वंश बढ़कर उन्हींके नामसे सीसोदियोंकी शाखा मशहूरहैं जिनका ज़िक्र मेवाड़के सर्दारोंके हालमें लिखा जायगा.

* श्यामलदास रचित *वीर विनोद* से उद्धृत

Annexure 4:
Ranawats of Sadri and their Lineage (Part 1)

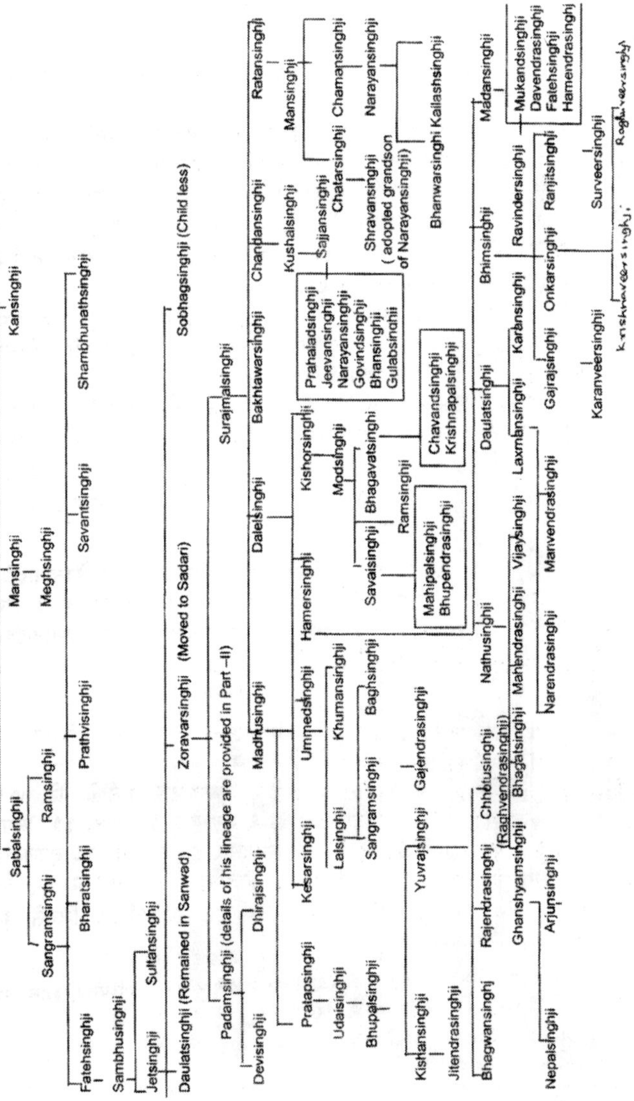

Annexure 4: Ranawats of Sadri and their Lineage (Part 2)

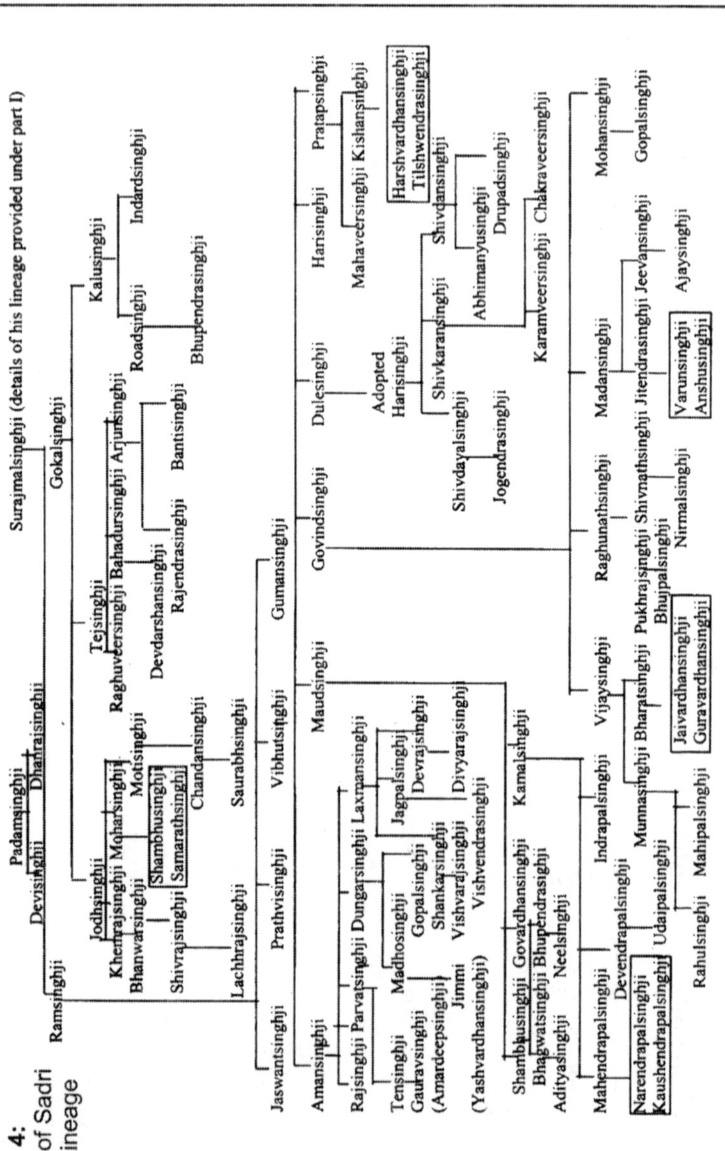

Annexure 5: Housing Patterns of Different Castes (Part 1)

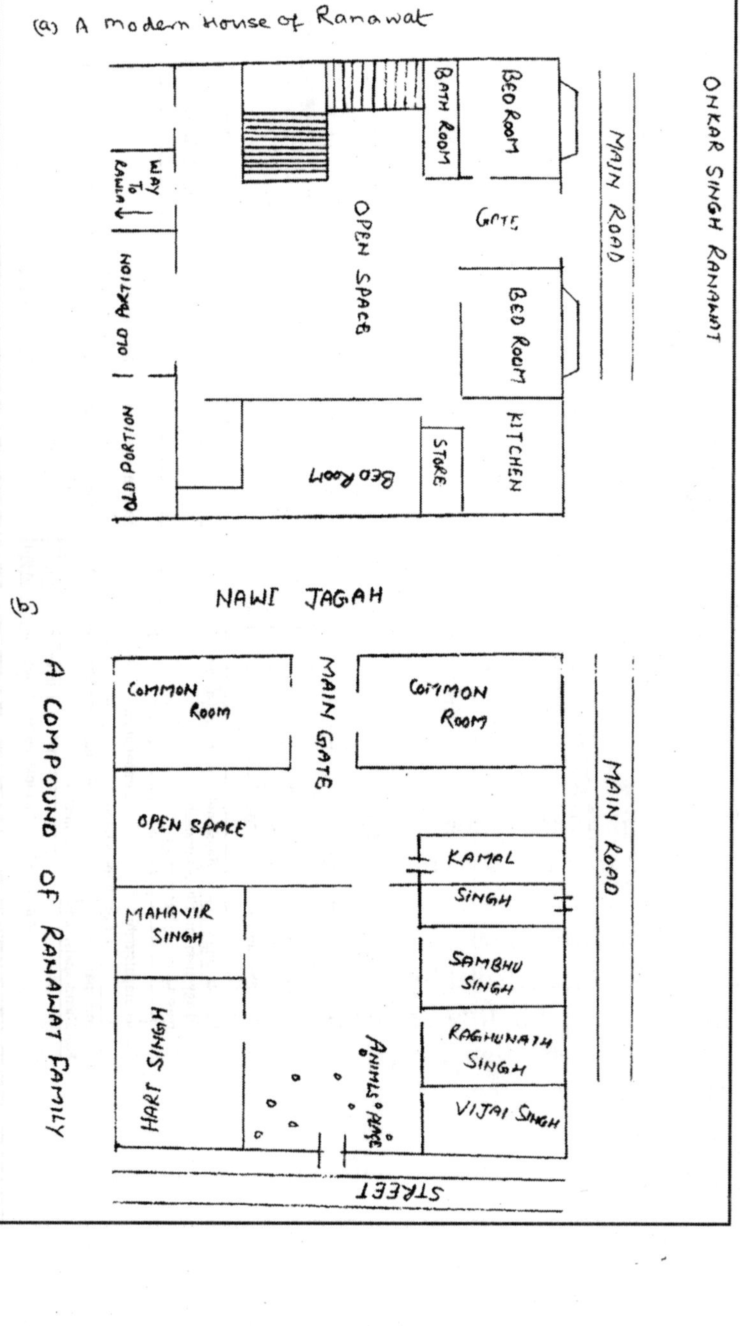

Annexure 5: Housing Patterns of Different Castes (Part 2)

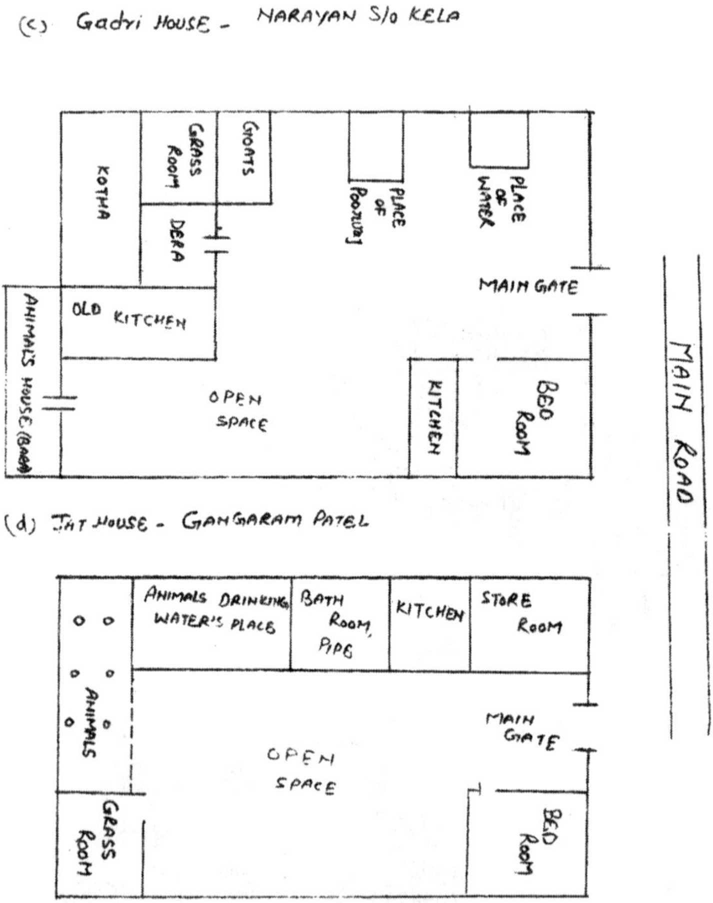

Photos 1955 / 2004

Surroundings for Data Collection

1955

2004

Transport

1955

2004

Housing

1955

2004

Economy and Technology

1955

2004

Religious Practices and Village Deities

1955

2004

Village Marriages

1955

2004

Obituaries and Tributes

Brij Raj Chauhan

1 March 1927 – 3 November 2009

Obituary: Brij Raj Chauhan*

Yogesh Atal

In the early hours of the 3 November 2009, Professor Brij Raj Chauhan, aged 82 years 8 months, breathed his last in Udaipur, Rajasthan. It is this city where he spent his childhood as part of the family that migrated from a small village in Western Uttar Pradesh, and where he returned after graduation from Lucknow to be the first lecturer in sociology in the state of Rajasthan in the year 1949. After his stints at Agra Institute of Social Sciences and at the Meerut University, he finally returned to Udaipur to resume his work and to retire. Udaipur became his exit door.

Though formally retired from the Meerut University in 1987, he was still at his desk computer – penning his work when his health fully failed him this year. A life totally devoted to sociology, nay social sciences, finally departed. Several generations of his students spread throughout the

* *The Eastern Anthropolgist*, Vol. 62, No. 4, October–December 2009, pp. 537–39.

country and abroad lost their mentor and a father-figure – fondly called *Dadda* by many of his students.

Professor Chauhan was a product of Lucknow Department of Economics which pioneered teaching of Sociology and Anthropology disregarding disciplinary barriers. He carried that flame to Rajasthan when the introduction of sociology at the B.A. level coincided with his return from Lucknow. He abandoned the idea of practising law and accepted the appointment at the local Government College to teach Sociology. As a pioneer he laid the foundations of the discipline in Rajasthan. It was mainly due to his efforts that M.A. courses in sociology at the Rajasthan University were introduced in 1957. Till then he encouraged some of his students to go to other campuses outside of Rajasthan for postgraduate studies.

To create a favourable climate for the subject in the state he organised Rajasthan Sociological Conferences and succeeded in bringing to Udaipur luminaries such as K.M. Kapadia, S.C. Dube, M.S. Gore, and I.P. Desai, among others, to interact with his students.

Not only did he pioneer teaching of Sociology in Rajasthan, he also encouraged field studies in the rural hinterland. He himself carried out sustained field work in one of the villages for many years and produced a superb monograph on *A Rajasthan Village* that earned him a Ph.D. degree in social anthropology. He went to the University of California to spend a year with Kingsley Davis and develop expertise in social demography.

Before going to the United States, he spent a year at Sagar, and returned to Udaipur to become the first Director of the Tribal Research Institute. In 1964, he left Udaipur for good to join the Institute of Social Sciences at

Agra, from where he moved to the newly created Department of Sociology at the Meerut University in the early 1970s and worked there until his retirement in 1987. University Grants Commission awarded him the prestigious National Fellowship for the Year 1982.

With missionary zeal, he worked to promote sociology as a profession. He became a life member of the Indian Sociological Society soon after its establishment, and he also participated in the All India Sociological conferences – the former was at the initiative of the Bombay School and the latter of the Lucknow School. At a later date, the two initiatives were merged and the Conference became an activity of the Indian Sociological Society. He was also instrumental in creating the U.P. Sociological Society. It is to his credit that he organised two sessions of the All India Sociological Conference, one at Meerut and another at Udaipur. Being a student of Professor D.N. Majumdar, he was associated with the Ethnographic and Folk Culture Society [EFCS], and contributed to its Journal, *The Eastern Anthropologist*; in fact, he recently guest-edited a special volume on Village Studies for EA.

Professor Chauhan is perhaps the only one who had attended almost all the sessions of the All India Sociological Conferences, and of EFCS; and he also enlisted participation of his peers and students in them. He served for a term as the President of the Indian Sociological Society. At the time of the 2008 All India Sociological Conference, he was awarded Lifetime Achievement Plaque in Jaipur which he went personally to receive, despite his indifferent health. Alas! that was his last. At the time of Srinagar Conference, held in October 2009, he was bed-ridden with multiple problems and he bid adieu to the world soon after.

Besides being an organization man, Professor Chauhan was a teacher *par excellence*. He invested his energies and time both in strengthening the professional association and in grooming the young sociologists. He taught not only in the narrow precincts of a class room but extra-murally as well. His company was a learning experience. Students got gems of knowledge while promenading with him; serendipitously, they were made to notice points of significance in a seemingly routine happening. He always regarded Participant Observation as the strongest tool with the social sciences. That is why he used to take students to villages for field work. He took students on tours to distant places such as Kerala and Nepal. He did not spare even the foreign social scientists visiting him from the arduous task of travelling to the villages to get first hand exposure to rural life. For him, the villages studied by his seniors and peers were centres of pilgrim. Perhaps he is the only sociologist who has revisited all such places be it Rampura of Srinivas, Gohana Kalan of Majumdar, Shamirpet of Dube, Rankhandi and Jhaberan of the Cornell-India team, or Kheri of Atal. His last trip on his way to Udaipur from Bhopal was to a village in Dewas studied in the 1950s by Adrian Mayer.

Professor Chauhan authored several articles and books both in English and Hindi. His publications include *A Rajasthan Village* (1967, and 1999), *Towns in the Tribal Setting* (1970); *Scheduled Castes and Education* (1975); *Bharat Mein Grameen Samaj* (1988); *India: A Socio-Economic Profile* (1989); *Rural-Urban Articulations* (1991); *Samaj Vigyan Ke Prerak Srot* (1994); and *Rural Life: Grass Roots Perspectives* (2009). With his student, Satyanarayan Alturi, he nearly completed another anthology of essays on rural India, titled *Village Life: Events and Dimensions*, which will now be posthumously published. He was also contemplating to do some more books, and was constantly enquiring from his students about the progress on their projects. Only a few days prior to his death he phoned me to inform of his satisfaction on the publication of ICSSR *Survey of Sociology and Social Anthropology* (fourth round) that I had edited. And he enquired about the progress on my present project of doing a textbook on Sociology for South Asia.

Saintly and self-effacing, this Khadi-clad scholar remained fully devoted to the social sciences, disregarding the fruitless debate on the distinction between sociology and anthropology. A dedicated field worker, an erudite scholar, and a remarkable teacher, Professor Chauhan's departure has created a void.

His students will remain indebted to him; the only way to repay the debt to him is to carry his tradition of hard work, commitment to the social sciences, and training the coming generation of students to become good sociologists.

My tearful obeisance to the person with whom I had an association of more than 56 years during which not only did I receive from him scholarly guidance and encouragement but also filial affection and blessings. His death is a severe personal loss to me and my family.

Yogesh Atal

Brij Raj Chauhan: A Personal Tribute

*Surendra Munshi**

Many years ago when a common German friend introduced me to M.N. Srinivas in Singapore, he asked me about my academic background. I was associated at that time with Sociological Research Unit of the Indian Statistical Institute in Calcutta. Having studied philosophy for my graduation in Calcutta, I studied at the Institute of Social Sciences in Agra for my master's degree in sociology. He took note of my having studied at Agra and asked me why I had gone there and quite explicitly asked me why I had not studied in Delhi. I frankly told him I landed in Agra after it turned out that admissions in his department in Delhi had closed. Having said this, I added that I was happy it had worked out in that manner.

Srinivas reacted in disbelief. I further explained that I had a clear reason for saying so. Had I studied in Delhi I would have learnt to do sociology in one style, whereas

* Retired Professor of Sociology, Indian Institute of Management, Calcutta.

studying in Agra I was exposed to doing sociology in different styles.

This was indeed my honest assessment and it remains so to this date. Institute of Social Sciences in Agra in the years I studied there – 1965 to 1967 – was a rich place for studying sociology. I was exposed there to social anthropology (Brij Raj Chauhan), Marxism and more (B.D. Soni), formal sociology (D.N. Dhanagare), and American sociology (Yogesh Atal), not to forget a talented group of statisticians, headed by D.D. Joshi. Class sizes in both years were small, and the university library in the park was reasonably good. Above all, the teachers of the department were enthusiastic and treated students well. With all their differences of orientation, they were open to discussions with each other and with students. I did not ever feel that there were sectarian concerns or personal rivalries. Presiding over this happy group was Chauhan Saheb whose room with an open door was available to his colleagues. We saw them meet there regularly, full of discussions and good will. When I look back at those years, I think I took from this talented quartet, teaching us sociology together, a sense of openness to different ways of doing sociology.

What did I take from Chauhan Saheb in particular? This is a difficult question to answer, for I took from him much, not all of it can be easily identified.

I took from him clearly an awareness of a different India. Having been brought up in Calcutta, I was unaware of what rural India, especially in north India, meant. Chauhan Saheb could draw from his study of a Rajasthan village and his own rural background to make this part of India come alive for us. His study bears reading even today. It is true that he was advised by D.N. Majumdar to carry out his study as that of a little community[1] and current trends in rural sociology have gone beyond such a conception. We should at the same time keep in mind that he saw across different villages, highlighting *Chokhala* which he defined as the unit of a caste or sub-caste that goes beyond a village and covers a number of contiguous villages which bind the members of the caste to some collective regulations. Nor did he overlook power dimensions in villages.[2] I find his study '*The Panchayati Raj and the Democratic Polity*' instructive insofar as he provides here an analysis based not only on a consideration of the concepts under discussion but also an overview of the historical growth of local self-governing institutions in India, drawing out implications of such institutions for a democratic order.[3] His study of the *Towns in the Tribal Setting*, moreover, made an early attempt to identify the process of the diffusion of 'urban elements' through an intensive study of selected villages and towns.[4]

As far as his approach to village India is concerned, I was struck by the lack of any caste prejudice in a person whose origins were clearly from an upper caste from the rural milieu.[5] The Brij Raj-ji Chauhan of the village Chak-Salempur, who studied in his privileged school meant for princely families in Rajasthan thought about Scheduled Castes and Tribes. He wrote on them with concern. I find his article on Scheduled Castes and Tribes, published in 1969, exemplary in more than one sense.[6] In writing this tribute, I have searched and looked at my empirical research report which I submitted as part of my M.A. examination requirement. It was a study conducted under the overall direction of Chauhan Saheb on the theme of untouchability in an urban setting with the title,

'A Study of Jatavs in Agra City'. It was carried out in a locality situated practically near a gutter. I found that, while there were formal interactions with other occupational castes such as washer men and barbers, the Jatavs of the locality were largely confined to themselves in their primary social relations.

This brings me to the second point regarding what I took from Chauhan Saheb. It was his emphasis on *method*. He was much concerned with honing our skills as researchers. Participant observation was, of course, his strong point. He was clear about its usefulness in the training of a sociologist. This did not close him to appreciating the value of other methods. I have already indicated how in writing about the *Panchayati Raj* he considered history, drawing from ancient texts and modern sources. Moreover, not many realise the kind of competence he had in dealing with demographic data. A look at his article on Scheduled Castes and Tribes should convince anyone that the year he spent with Kingsley Davis at the University of California was not wasted.

Less tangible, but more important, learning for me was the joy of cultivating an inquiring mind. This man of simple appearance was blessed with a sophisticated intellect. I was fortunate to find acceptance by him, not only in his office room but also at his home. Indeed, even more, on the streets of Agra. Atal Saheb who had an earlier and longer association with him has mentioned how he learnt his sociology walking with him on the streets of Udaipur. I learnt my sociology walking with him on the streets of Agra later. These walks, long walks, had a peculiar character. He would usually begin with a question on what I was thinking currently. This used to be a serious question, for he would listen to me with attention. That would give rise to a dialogue – questions, answers, doubts, more doubts, and some clarifications. As I look back at these dialogues, I am struck by the fact that there was no hierarchy in these dialogues, no take it from me from a teacher to a student. There was a serious effort to understand sociology and its concerns and what sense it made to understand the life around us. These walks with him are my closest experience of what it might have been like for the young and inexperienced men of Athens to be with Socrates.

With some experience now, I can reason that such a handling of a student could not have been possible if he were not at heart himself an eternal student. If he became a *Guru* or made a fetish of what he had learnt from a *Guru* – Indian or foreign, he could not have engaged in such a dialogue. Only an eternal student could acknowledge openly what he learnt from others. Consider, for example, what he has to say on Soni Saheb, another remarkable person. In the closing part of his autobiographical note he lists his debts to him. 'One of the few persons', as he observes, 'whose seriousness in the discipline would remain little known beyond the small group!'[7]

I met Chauhan Saheb last in Udaipur in the winter of 2003. He was busy with the sociological conference then and was not in good health. Yet, he found time for me. He began with his usual question on what I was thinking currently. And then we had a dialogue.

Notes

1. For this and other biographical information I draw from his delightful essay 'Rural Ingredients and Exposures: An

Autobiographical Note' in Brij Raj Chauhan, *Rural Life: Grass Roots Perspectives*, New Delhi, Concept Publishing Company, 2009, pp. 59–86.

2. Brij Raj Chauhan, 'Intervillage Organization of a Caste in Rajasthan', *Sociological Bulletin*, Vol. 13, No. 2, 1964, pp. 24–35
3. Brij Raj Chauhan, 'The Panchayati Raj and the Democratic Polity', *Sociological Bulletin*, Vol. 17, No. 1, 1968, pp. 35–54.
4. Brij Raj Chauhan, *Towns in the Tribal Setting*, Delhi, National Publishing House, 1970.
5. Lack of caste prejudice by a person of the upper caste is not to be taken for granted. See: Surendra Munshi, 'Tribal Absorption and Sanskritization in Hindu Society', *Contributions to Indian Sociology*, Vol. 13, No. 2, 1979, pp. 293–317.
6. Brij Raj Chauhan, 'Scheduled Castes and Tribes', *Economic and Political Weekly*, Vol. 4, No. 4, 1969, pp. 257–63.
7. *An Autobiographical Note*, p. 85.

Remembering Professor Brij Raj Chauhan

*Jagdish Kumar Pundir**

For me, remembering Professor Brij Raj Chauhan is possible only by alluding to my interactions with him over the years in an autobiographic manner.

I met Professor Chauhan for the first time in his chamber at Meerut University campus during the summer of 1975 when I was preparing for my M.A.(sociology) final year examination as a private student. While receiving me, he raised his head, took off his spectacles and put them aside on the table. His eyes gave me the impression that he had read everything about me. The deep eye-to-eye contact also created a sense of fear in my mind. This was a short rendezvous; not much of conversation.

After a couple of months later, I came to the university again, and went to his chamber to tell him of my desire to take admission in M.Phil. With great efforts I could utter the words: "Sir I have got the gate pass to come to you (my career record was good enough for admission

* Formerly Professor of Sociology, CCS University, Meerut.

to M.Phil. as per new norms) but neither I know sociology nor English language to cope with the studies of the course." He just said, "you may do if you are willing." That became an important event of my life and marked the beginning of my learning a little of both, Sociology as well as English under his tutelage.

On the very first occasion of his class lecture, in an afternoon, knowing that I hail from a village, he gave us the assignment to write one page about our village. I was surprised to note the assignment, as I could not understand that this was the first lesson of doing field work based on participant observation and reporting in the area of rural sociology. After taking admission, I went back to my village and came back after eighteen or nineteen days. On the very first day, after the class, he asked me to stay for a moment. He said, "you may be interested in getting a lectureship, you may join that, there are vacancies in the degree colleges or some scholarships have been approved for M.Phil. scholars; you may as well continue the course with that." To my utter surprise, I gathered the courage to immediately react 'sir I have come here to learn and stay under your supervision at least for one year.' He said 'welcome but please think and tell me tomorrow.' Probably from that day his face never appeared frightened me, unlike some other students. This marked the first lesson of my learning experience and presentation. Finding readings difficult particularly reading all books in English, he suggested that I should start reading An *Indian village* authored by S.C. Dube). Later, he advised me to read B. Malinowski and Radcliffe-Brown's writings. The small assignments continued as also my interaction with him, somewhat on every working day. He was the founder of Sociology at Meerut University (1970). Likewise, he was the initiator of sociological understanding, particularly of rural society, among his students. He designed course of M.Phil. in such a way that gradual learning was built into it. In the very first semester, a course (out of five) was solely based on fieldwork. His brief and slow direction was to observe (see) and write and discuss. Another course was also of the kind in which we had to submit a term paper based exclusively on the survey/review of literature (Sociological Abstracts). In the second semester, he advised us to take an optional course on 'Area study of Nepal'. We did not know that his heuristic method of teaching and our learning process was so deeply built into it. He was of the firm opinion that more we see the different places and meet varieties of people the more our understanding and vision would grow through such exposures. We understood this during later years.

When M.A. was started in the department, he prescribed for every semester some practical exercises related to some course contents, based either on a little field work or some library work, e.g. secondary sources of data. In one such exercise, I was deputed to go and live with students in one of the two 'India's changing villages' (S.C. Dube), namely, the village of Rankhandi in Saharanpur district. Later on, this exercise resulted into a research paper 'Rankhandi: The Village Elites' based on the seven case studies completed with the group of students. These lessons of learning – teaching were integrated with small research/fieldwork exercises. I am one of those privileged students of Professor Chauhan who has grown through these experiences under his guidance. I prepared a paper based on the experiences for a seminar organized at the time of his farewell in October 1987. The same paper titled, 'Integrating Research

Methods with teaching in Sociology' was later published in an important journal.

Wherever and whenever Professor Chauhan had time he thought of sociology and of his students. But all the students were not so receptive. Working with him required patience, some thinking and some additional hard work. During the later years, when our interactions increased, he stated that 'only some pass the test of becoming sincere and I interact with them more and for longer-period.' As some of us still remember his teachings were better outside the classroom when we used to walk with him in the evenings, taking tea in a small shop away from home and department. During M.Phil. second semester in May 1976 when we were almost ready to go for field work of 2–3 weeks in Nepal under the Area Study Programme with him, he had a mild heart attack. Consequently he was admitted to Moolchand Hospital in New Delhi. During his hospital days also, he was thinking of some new programmes of development to be studied by students of sociology. It was this hospital stay which gave me the idea of a topic which I persued for my M.Phil. and Ph.D. dissertations.

There have been several such occasions, particularly in my career in sociology in the initial years, that gave rise to important pieces of research. During the field study for my M.Phil., and later when I shared notes with him, as he was always keen to know whenever any of his students came back from the field, some new ideas sprung in his mind. He asked me to write a page about each one of the four events. I could not understand why he was saying this but I penned down. After two days when I brought those four pages, he asked me 'what comes out of these when you put them together in a time sequence? Write down the outcome.' When the findings were written, he said 'It is the answer (conclusion), now raise a question and write with some background in the beginning.' Next day he said, 'it is a research paper, now ready' and gave me a circular of a conference of Criminology which was going to be held after three weeks. He asked me to match the theme of the paper with a sub theme of the conference and to send it to the Conference organisers. Later, that small paper was published by some political scientist in a volume. That was a paper which was posted on Google for many years.

Last instance I remember when he was on a fellowship of ICSSR at G. B. Pant Institute, Allahabad. He was then compiling a volume of rural studies in Uttar Pradesh. He asked me to find out a paper (based on my field work for M.Phil.) which I had presented some thirty years ago but was not published. Knowing my capabilities and habits more than I know myself, he stated 'you will have that in some of your files, edit the same and send it to me.' He published it in the volume.

Such were his methods of teaching and learning for those who had some patience and curiosity to learn. He may be one who realized how creativity can be inspired in the minds of the upcoming younger generation. On the occasion of his farewell in 1987, one of the senior sociologists present on the occasion said, 'Professor Brij Raj Chauhan is a sociologist of sociological imagination'. Such was his life pattern as a teacher – sociologist. Long live his memories with us.

My Guru Chauhan Saheb

Jainendra Kumar Doshi

Though time runs out fast memories of my interactions with Chauhan Saheb have remained ever fresh. If he were alive today he would be nine decades old. I sometime deliberate, how was he different from other teachers that he does not fad out of memory. He taught sociology but his approach to his students was holistic. He taught sociology but encouraged his students to excel in sports and games as well. He himself had played cricket, a good sports commentator. It was somewhat unusual that an academician of his calibre was also a sports commentator. He created history when he made a century in the Ranji Trophy Tournament.

I came in his contact a bit late as I changed over from commerce to arts after my intermediate. Probably, I was forced to study commerce against my wishes. I felt more comfortable when I joined BA with Sociology as one of the optionals. Professor Chauhan did not take much time in realizing my potential and encouraged me at every step to

---

J.K. Doshi retired in 1998 from G.B. Pant University of Agriculture and Technology, Pantnagar, UP, now in Uttarakhand.

make a career in social sciences. Soon after my graduation, he saw to it that I along with two other students followed the foot prints of our senior Yogesh Atal who had opted to move to Sagar University. I, alongwith Gopal Bhardwaj and Ravi Dutt Sharma went to Sagar for our post-graduation. It so happened that when we were in the final year, Professor Dube succeeded in bringing Professor Chauhan to join his faculty. Professor Dube, being a very reputed social scientist, was often on move; hence, during that period professor Chauhan filled the vacuum. Professor Chauhan, though quiet by nature, was academically very active, as well as articulate. As a result, after a short stint at Sagar, he went back to Udaipur, and then appointed at the Institute of Social Sciences of the Agra University. Finally he moved to Meerut as the founding Professor of Sociology in the newly established University. Though I too changed several jobs working at Indian Institute of Mass Communications in Delhi, National Institute of Rural Development, and G.B. Pant University, Allahabad, I always kept myself in contact with him and interacted intellectually.

Unlike many professional colleagues of Professor Chauhan, he never broke away from his roots. He always found opportunity to visit his students regularly. He remained simple, always accessible and down to earth. He had several students who held very senior positions in academia and government.

Today Chauhan Saheb is physically not with us but most of my generation recalls their association with him with nostalgia. I recall his habit of drinking tea with his friends, colleagues, and even students. We used to joke not how many cups but how many kettles of tea in a day he relishes. His rapport with his students was *par excellence*. I recall on weekends or holidays he would sit with his students and listen to their presentations. He would sometimes cut jokes too but they were also academic in their import. Not only in the classrooms but also on busy streets he found occasion to explain the key concepts by picking up local examples. That constantly reminded us that sociology is not esoteric.

He is not physically with us today but I can hear his laughter; I can feel his presence. I recall a few occasions in Sagar when I was depressed, not getting money order from home for my monthly expenses, or feeling not happy with my performance in class. I knew, he used to support financially some students who had problems in continuing their studies for failure to pay fee.

He quietly helped needy students financially. His involvement with his students was that of a friend, philosopher and guide. He had been a student of the pioneering anthropologist, Professor D.N. Majumdar in Lucknow University. Professor Chauhan loved to do field work himself and motivated his students also to work in tribal and rural areas. He was very simple in his living. He always encouraged and motivated his students to explore new avenues. In one word, he was a teacher few could match. I feel very nostalgic when I recall days of my association with him.

Today, Chauhan Saheb is no longer with us but memories of his presence linger on. He was one teacher who even after his physical departure from amidst us remains with us.

Index